Second Corinthians

INTERPRETATION
BIBLE STUDIES

Genesis, CELIA BREWER SINCLAIR

Exodus, JAMES D. NEWSOME JR.

First and Second Samuel, DAVID C. HESTER

Esther and Ruth, PATRICIA K. TULL

Job, DAVID C. HESTER

Psalms, JEROME F. D. CREACH

Isaiah, GARY W. LIGHT

Jeremiah, ROBERT R. LAHA JR.

Matthew, ALYCE M. McKENZIE

Mark, RICHARD I. DEIBERT

Luke, THOMAS W. WALKER

John, MARK A. MATSON

Acts, CHARLES C. WILLIAMSON

Romans, ART ROSS AND MARTHA M. STEVENSON

First Corinthians, BRUCE N. FISK

Second Corinthians, WILLIAM M. RAMSAY

Philippians and Galatians, STANLEY P. SAUNDERS

Hebrews, EARL S. JOHNSON, JR.

Revelation, WILLIAM C. PENDER

Second Corinthians

WILLIAM M. RAMSAY

WESTMINSTER
JOHN KNOX PRESS
LOUISVILLE · KENTUCKY

First edition
Published by Westminster John Knox Press
Louisville, Kentucky

13 14 15 16 17 18 19 20 21 22—10 9 8 7 6 5 4 3 2

Book design by Drew Stevens
Cover design by Pam Poll
Cover illustration by Robert Stratton

Library of Congress Cataloging-in-Publication Data
Ramsay, William M.
　Second Corinthians / William M. Ramsay.—1st ed.
　　p. cm. — (Interpretation Bible studies)
　Includes bibliographical references.
　ISBN 0-664-22637-X (alk. paper)
　1. Bible. N.T. Corinthians, 2nd—Criticism, interpretation, etc. 2. Bible, N.T. Corinthians, 2nd—Textbooks. I. Title. II. Series.
　BS2675.52.R35 2004
　227'.307—dc22

　　　　　　　　　　　　　　　　　　　　　　　　　　　　　　　2003057659

Most Westminster John Knox Press books are available at special quantity
discounts when purchased in bulk by corporations, organizations, and special-interest
groups. For more information, please e-mail SpecialSales@wjkbooks.com.

Contents

Series Introduction

The Bible has long been revered for its witness to God's presence and redeeming activity in the world; its message of creation and judgment, love and forgiveness, grace and hope; its memorable characters and stories; its challenges to human life; and its power to shape faith. For generations people have found in the Bible inspiration and instruction, and, for nearly as long, commentators and scholars have assisted students of the Bible. This series, Interpretation Bible Studies (IBS), continues that great heritage of scholarship with a fresh approach to biblical study.

Designed for ease and flexibility of use for either personal or group study, IBS helps readers not only to learn about the history and theology of the Bible, understand the sometimes difficult language of biblical passages, and marvel at the biblical accounts of God's activity in human life, but also to accept the challenge of the Bible's call to discipleship. IBS offers sound guidance for deepening one's knowledge of the Bible and for faithful Christian living in today's world.

IBS was developed out of three primary convictions. First, the Bible is the church's scripture and stands in a unique place of authority in Christian understanding. Second, good scholarship helps readers understand the truths of the Bible and sharpens their perception of God speaking through the Bible. Third, deep knowledge of the Bible bears fruit in one's ethical and spiritual life.

Each IBS volume has ten brief units of key passages from a book of the Bible. By moving through these units, readers capture the sweep of the whole biblical book. Each unit includes study helps, such as maps, photos, definitions of key terms, questions for reflection, and suggestions for resources for further study. In the back of each volume is a Leader's Guide that offers helpful suggestions on how to use IBS.

The Interpretation Bible Studies series grows out of the well-known Interpretation commentaries (Westminster John Knox Press), a series that helps preachers and teachers in their preparation. Although each IBS volume bears a deep kinship to its companion Interpretation commentary, IBS can stand alone. The reader need not be familiar with the Interpretation commentary to benefit from IBS. However, those who want to discover even more about the Bible will benefit by consulting Interpretation commentaries too.

Through the kind of encounter with the Bible encouraged by the Interpretation Bible Studies, the church will continue to discover God speaking afresh in the scriptures.

Introduction to 2 Corinthians

Readers of 2 Corinthians are likely to agree that Peter was right about Paul's letters: "There are some things in them hard to understand" (2 Pet. 3:16). That is the bad news, but there is good news: First, this commentary will help explain some of those hard things. Also, there is so much in 2 Corinthians that is delightful and inspiring that even if it takes a little study you will find it well worth while. Here are just a few of the things that make this such a great book that for centuries Christians have said it deserves to be thought of as part of the very word of God.

1. Its promises of a glorious life planned for us after death are so comforting that they are read at millions of funerals. Remember that they were written to give people courage not just in death but in life.

> "It's not the things in the Bible I don't understand; it's what I do understand that bothers me."—attributed to Mark Twain.

2. Paul uses delightful, thought-provoking figures of speech about us. He calls us *letters of Christ*, God's *perfume, clay pots*—but full of gospel treasure—and *ambassadors* on Christ's royal mission.
3. Paul himself gives us an example of humility and proper self-respect, as well as the most remarkable autobiography ever written by any saint and future martyr.
4. Second Corinthians 8 and 9 contain the world's best stewardship messages.
5. And . . . well, there is lots more, as you will see.

The Cast of Characters

If this were an actual drama instead of a dramatic letter, the following would compose the cast of characters. First, there is the *church* at

Corinth. Read Acts 18:1–21 for the story of how Paul preached there, the synagogue split, a church was established, and Paul was almost lynched. We already know from 1 Corinthians that the Corinthian church members were a rowdy bunch, given to feuding with each other. They included a few rich members who wouldn't wait for the slaves and day laborers to get off from work, but who would instead go ahead and eat the best things at the church suppers. There were tongues speakers and others who talked in the service all at once so that nobody understood. There were some who were sexually immoral, some who had odd views about the resurrection, some who were stingy, and some women whom Paul, at least, regarded as uppity. The church at Corinth was an interesting mixture of "saints"!

We also see *enemies* of Paul in the Corinthian church, intruders trying to undermine Paul's work. Sarcastically Paul calls them "super-apostles." Attacking Paul, they claimed to be stricter Jews, better Christians, more eloquent preachers, and more effective apostles. They also claimed that the gospel they preached, not Paul's, was the truth.

There are some relatively *minor characters*. Titus served Paul as a go-between when at one time it seemed to Paul that he had better not return to Corinth. Timothy had helped found the church at Corinth. Paul associates Timothy with himself as he writes this letter. Finally, there is an unknown Corinthian who had somehow deeply hurt Paul.

At the center, of course, is *Paul himself.* Nobody knows what he looked like. By the time he wrote 2 Corinthians, his back must have been a mass of scars, and so many bones had been broken that he must have been crippled with arthritis. Read 2 Corinthians 11:23–28 for a brief summary of the battering he had gone through. A second-century historical novel called *The Acts of Paul and Thecla* imagines him like this:

> a man small in size, bald-headed, bow legged, with meeting eyebrows, a large, red, and somewhat hooked nose, strongly built, he was full of friendliness, *for at times he looked like a man, at times like an angel.* (As quoted in Ramsay 1994, 381, italics added)

We will see him in this letter sometimes looking perhaps all too much "like a man," but often something shines through that makes him seem quite "like an angel."

2 CORINTHIANS
Paul's Ministry—and Their Partnership in It

| 1:1 | 10:1 | 13:14 |

A Joyful Letter in Response to Titus's Report: Paul and the Corinthians are Reconciled, Partners Again in Ministry

A review of how Paul had been distressed over the apparent rejection of him, and his joy at the news of reconciliation Titus had brought, 1–2

Paul's ministry, in which confidence is renewed and in which the Corinthians are partners again, 3:1–4:12

The encouragement in that ministry that comes from the eschatological hope, 4:13–5:21

A plea for continued partnership in ministry, in spite of difficulties, 6:1–7:4 (6:14–7:1 is a parenthesis on some who are excluded from that partnership.)

Picking up from chapter 2, Paul's joy in the good news of reconciliation Titus has brought, 7:2–16

A plea for financial partnership in ministry to the poor of the Jerusalem church, 8–9

A Severe Letter Defending Paul's Ministerial Authority as an Apostle against Attacks Being Spread in Corinth

Paul's apology for defending ("boasting of") his authority, 1:10–11:21a

The signs that Paul really has apostolic authority:
his credentials as a good Jew, 11:21b–22
his sacrifices for Christ, 11:23–33
his religious experiences, 12:1–10
his miracles and mighty works, 12:11–13

A plea that they repent and accept his authority before his coming visit, 12:14–13:13

Author: Paul

Recipients: The church he had founded in Corinth

Date: About A.D. 53–54

Occasion: Chapters 1–9 grow out of a report from Titus that the Corinthian church is ready again to work with Paul in ministry. All is well again. Chapters 10–13 reflect serious attacks on Paul that have spread in Corinth.

Purpose: 1–9: To rejoice and to encourage the church in mutual ministry with Paul 10–13: Desperately to seek to reestablish Paul's authority before he visits them

William M. Ramsay, *The Westminster Guide to the Books of the Bible* (Louisville, Ky.: Westminster John Knox Press, 1994).

The Story behind the Letter

The plot of the drama is clear: Paul is fighting to save his standing and his gospel against intruders who are undermining his reputation and work. The sequence of events that are the background of the drama, however, is not so clear. With a bit of digging you can discover some things. We know from Acts 18 about Paul's first visit to Corinth. We also have a long letter he wrote back to the church there, which the Bible preserves as 1 Corinthians. That epistle mentions an even earlier letter (1 Cor. 5:9). Evidently he made another visit to Corinth, a painful one (2 Cor. 2:1), a visit not recorded in Acts. He found people attempting to subvert his work, and one person in particular deeply offended Paul (2:5–11). In that controversy he got little support from the church. He wrote at least one other letter, one so full of rebuke that at times he wished he had not sent it (2:3; 7:8). He planned more visits but felt led to postpone them (1:15–16; 2:1), lest he stir up even more distress.

Instead of going himself he sent Titus (2 Cor. 2:13). When Titus was slow returning, Paul was so anxious for news that he set out to find him. "But," he cries, "thanks be to God!" (2:14). Titus now had brought good news: Paul's enemy had been disciplined by the church, and the Corinthian Christians longed to see him again (7:5–7). All was forgiveness, peace, and comfort.

"This is the most personal of all Paul's letters, the one that most fully reveals his heart and purpose."—Floyd V. Filson and James Reid, *The Second Epistle to the Corinthians,* Interpreter's Bible 10 (Nashville: Abingdon Press, 1953), 268.

So does the story have a happy ending? The last chapters (10–13) show us a very human Paul defending himself against all kinds of attacks and, in turn, attacking his enemies with bitter sarcasm. Perhaps, many have suggested, those chapters are part of the earlier painful letter mentioned in 2 Corinthians 7:8. Those chapters are placed last, however, and the painful letter may have been focused on one person more than on the whole church. Acts implies that Paul did finally make that visit he had planned (Acts 19:21; 20:2–3; 2 Cor. 13:1).

One thing we know for sure: Some folks in Corinth so loved and revered Paul that they collected some of his letters and saved them for us. Thus, for us at least, the drama has a happy ending.

Many scholars think that 2 Corinthians is made up of parts of several letters. Page 3 has an outline for 2 Corinthians in the form we have it.

On Using This Commentary

Never forget: This commentary is not a substitute for 2 Corinthians itself. Read with the Bible in one hand and this book in the other. It will go slowly over some high points of 2 Corinthians, skimming more quickly through some other parts. It is a briefer companion piece for the more detailed and strongly recommended *Second Corinthians,* by Ernest Best, in the Interpretation Bible Commentary series (Atlanta: John Knox Press, 1987).

Finally, Peter was right about Paul's letters; some things in them are hard to understand. It is not essential, however, to put in correct order all the events and interpret perfectly all the parts of this letter. Paul pleads with the Corinthians, "Make room in your hearts for us." If you read 2 Corinthians not only with a discerning mind but with that "open heart," you will find in it the very word of God.

Want to Know More?

About 2 Corinthians? See J. Paul Sampley, *The Second Letter to the Corinthians,* New Interpreter's Bible 11 (Nashville: Abingdon Press, 2000); William Barclay, *The Letters to the Corinthians,* rev. ed., Daily Bible Study (Louisville, Ky.: Westminster John Knox Press, 2002); John Calvin, *The Second Epistle of Paul the Apostle to the Corinthians* (Grand Rapids: Wm. B. Eerdmans Publishing Company, 1964).

About Corinth? Searching for "Ancient Corinth" on the Web will give you articles and pictures.

About each individual named in the letter? See Ronald Brownrigg, *Who's Who in the New Testament* (New York: Holt, Rinehart & Winston, 1971).

About a fuller overview of 2 Corinthians? See William M. Ramsay, *The Westminster Guide to the Books of the Bible* (Louisville, Ky.: Westminster John Knox Press, 1994), 416–22.

1

2 Corinthians 1:1–22

Suffering and Encouragement

Sometime around A.D. 54 an itinerant tent-maker and evangelist dictated to his young assistant a letter to a church he had founded. This was at least the fourth time he had written them, and he had been back to see them at least once. That visit had been a disaster. Sick, angry, and depressed, he had written them one letter so full of bitterness that he had wished that it had never been sent.

Now, however, he has received good news: Angry as it was, the letter had been successful. The church member who had been most difficult had been disciplined, and reconciliation was taking place.

Encouraged by that report, Paul began another letter. Though he was well aware that he had authority from God, Paul had no thought that he was writing for the ages. Christians down through the centuries, however, have revered 2 Corinthians as an important part of the written

Corinth was an important Greek coastal city.

word of God, a word not just to Corinthians but to themselves. The first word Paul had for that disturbed church—and now for us—was "comfort" or "encouragement."

The Heading of the Letter (1:1-3)

Paul begins in the form that was conventional for letters in that time. He gives his name, then says to whom the letter is addressed, gives a greeting, and voices a brief prayer. What he pours into that standard mold, however, already begins to make this letter worth our study.

He identifies himself as "an apostle of Jesus Christ." That is, he is "one sent" by his Lord. There were twelve original "disciples" (students), eleven of whom, with others, were given the great commission and thus were sent to spread the word. Paul too has been sent, and he recognizes that other Christians may be "apostles" also (Rom. 16:7). His authority lies in his Spirit-led fulfilling of that apostolic commission.

He includes Timothy as his partner, even though the letter itself makes clear that the real author is simply Paul. Timothy probably served as secretary while Paul dictated. The mention of Timothy helps also to renew a tie. The church at Corinth would remember Timothy, for that young man, Paul's "loyal child in the faith" (1 Tim. 1:2), had been with him in the early days of the Corinthian church (Acts 18:5).

He is writing to the church at Corinth, the capital of the region in Greece called Achaia. Paul could have addressed them honestly: "You bunch of greedy, feuding, rebellious sinners." Instead he calls them "saints." To Paul, all Christians are saints, "holy," set apart because they know the good news.

In every one of Paul's letters he uses a double greeting: "grace" and "peace." Even today you may hear two Israelis, as they meet each other, say not "Hello" but "Peace" (in Hebrew, *shalom*). It means that one wishes the other not only peace but prosperity and welfare. *Shalom* is frequently used in the Old Testament. "Really, now, do you think the world will ever have peace?" I asked a study group. One saintly woman was caring for her beloved husband as he slowly sank deeper into Alzheimer's disease. "In a way, I think I already have that peace," she told us. Her kind of peace comes from the "grace of the Lord Jesus Christ."

If "peace" is an Old Testament greeting, "grace" is a New Testament greeting. It recalls the unmerited favor of God given through Christ. Paul will use that word again in the benediction that ends this epistle, and we still sing of God's "amazing grace."

The opening prayer is simply a brief exclamation of joy: "Blessed [praised] be . . . God." That God, however, is carefully distinguished from other gods. Most Corinthians were religious, worshiping at

Corinth's great temple to Aphrodite or at shrines to Isis or Demeter. In recent years Americans have become familiar with shrines to Allah, Buddha, and Krishna, and some Americans have a kind of one-size-fits-all god of the pledge of allegiance and public prayers. Paul's is a very distinctive God, however: "the God and Father of our Lord Jesus Christ." That title describes the uniqueness of this God. Paul's God, and ours, is the one to whom Jesus prayed, the one whom Jesus revealed, the one whom Jesus showed on the cross to be "the Father of mercies," and whom now Paul will describe as the giver of "consolation."

First Comes Affliction (1:3–9)

When Paul writes of comfort he does not mean that he has been comfortable! Five times in seven verses he uses the words "affliction" or "afflict," and three times he writes "suffering" or "suffer." Indeed he has been so "utterly, unbearably crushed" that he had "despaired of life itself." Nobody knows exactly what difficulty Paul is writing about. Perhaps he had been so ill that he nearly died. Perhaps he had had one of those beatings he describes later in this epistle (6:4–5).

One kind of affliction we know he had been experiencing: Paul was deeply distressed about what had occurred on his last visit to Corinth. He had felt "afflicted in every way—disputes without and fears within" (7:5). For more than a year and a half, he had been a pastor to those people, he had risked his life for them, and now they seemed to be rejecting him. He was "so . . . unbearably crushed" that he "despaired of life itself" (1:8). John Calvin paraphrases Paul in this verse as saying, "so that I thought life was gone, or at least I had very little hope of it remaining, as those are wont to feel who are shut up and see no way of escape."

> "The preacher's job is to comfort the afflicted and afflict the comfortable."— familiar saying among ministers.

Paul speaks in three ways of "the sufferings of Christ." There is first of all the humiliation and torture Christ went through for us. Christ's suffering is so "abundant" that in a way it has spilled over to Paul. Calvin speaks of that "abundance" as "beyond measure," like an overloaded ship that seems almost to sink. Thus the agonies Paul has gone through for the Corinthians and their Lord have been "the sufferings of Christ." There is also a third meaning: They share in the "sufferings of Christ," too. It was not easy to be a Christian in Corinth. You might have to give up your job if you worked for a construction firm building a temple or a sculptor making idols. You might antagonize your husband who wanted meat when you could no longer go to the butcher shop, where the meat had been offered to a pagan god. You were likely to be ridiculed by friends; and as for enemies . . . they had nearly lynched Sosthenes (Acts 18:17)! From Christ to Paul to ordinary Christians, those "sufferings of Christ" kept spilling over; they were indeed "abundant." As the old gospel hymn by Thomas Shepherd (1693) mourns:

Must Jesus bear the cross alone, and all the world go free?
No there's a cross for everyone, and there's a cross for me.

The Purpose of Suffering: Consolation (1:3–7)

Now comes the good news: "consolation." Count the number of times in this passage that the word "consolation"—or "console"— occurs. Over and over Paul glories in it. He has received consolation; now they will, too. Just as the sufferings of Christ were so abundant that some overflow to us, "so also our consolation is abundant through Christ" (1:5).

Paul can even find a purpose in his sufferings: It is "so that we may be able to console those who are in any affliction." There was a purpose in Christ's sufferings. "Because he himself was tested by what he suffered, he is able to help those who are being tested" (Heb. 2:18). Whatever difficulties Paul went through, Christ had been through even more. And now, having gone through what he has experienced, Paul can help his sisters and brothers in Corinth.

For example: I think of a woman, herself no longer young, who had been visiting in a nursing home to comfort a church member, now old and infirm. "I don't know whether I helped her," she later reported, "but she surely helped me!" Somehow those who experience affliction often comfort us best. Knowing that they "patiently endure" their share of suffering comforts Paul, too. Their patient endurance, he says, gives him hope.

Encouragement (1:3–7)

The word Paul uses for "consolation" is *paraklesis*. Its root meaning is literally "called to the side of." The beloved King James Version translates it "comfort." The word does mean that. But Paul is not comfortable, nor were the Corinthian Christians. The translation I like is "encouragement" and "encourage."

That word is used of Barnabas. The other Christians nicknamed him "son of *paraklesis.*" We can understand why. When others rejected the newly converted Paul, their former persecutor, it was Barnabas who stood beside him. When Paul rejected Mark, who had left him in an earlier missionary journey, it was Barnabas who stood by Mark, giving him another chance. There is one other of whom almost the same word is used. The night before he died, God's Son promised the disciples that his Father would send the *paraklete,* the Holy Spirit (John 14:26). That One is the source of true consolation and encouragement, for Barnabas, for Paul, for the Corinthians, and for us.

To grasp, then, the consolation or encouragement that Paul says may come to us through suffering, think of what the Holy Spirit does for us in times of distress. Think, too, of Barnabas, a human being filled with that Spirit, who was "called to be beside" others, encouraging them when they needed a friend.

> "Friends halve the sorrow and double the joy."—traditional saying.

Early in the third century Septimus Severis attempted to stamp out Christianity. Perpetua, soon to be a mother, was arrested. As she cried in the pains of childbirth her tormenters asked her how she would endure the even worse suffering of being thrown to wild beasts. "When I face the beasts," she replied, "there will be another who will live in me." She would not be alone. Her courage in the arena amazed the crowd and encouraged other Christians. She knew there was One "called to be beside" her.

Partners in Service (1:7–22)

"Called as Partners in Christ's Service"—Paul would like Jane Parker Huber's hymn. Paul thinks of the Corinthian Christians as partners with him in four ways:

1. They share with him in suffering.
2. They share with him in consolation and encouragement.
3. They are his partners in prayer: "you also join in helping us by your prayers" (1:11).
4. Plus, he wants them to join with him in boasting (1:14).

Paul has already described their partnership in trouble and encouragement. Now he mentions prayer. Perhaps few things had encouraged Paul more than the news Titus brought him that the church was praying for him. This kind of partnership means that "many will give thanks on our behalf for the blessing granted us through the prayers of many" (v. 11). Spreading the prayer spreads the joy. The whole church can feel that they have had a share as he resumes his ministry.

Paul wants them also to be partners with him in "boasting." Verse 12 introduces this word "boast." Boasting will be a repeated theme throughout the epistle, especially in chapters 10–13. If you are a parent you can understand something of how Paul feels about the church he has brought to birth. "You are our boast," he tells them. He is humbly proud of his spiritual children.

He also wants them to be proud of him, to look up to him and trust him as God's messenger. "I *hope* . . . that on the day of the Lord Jesus [the judgment day] we are your boast," he says (1:13–14, emphasis added). Though apparently Paul has received reassuring news from Titus (7:6–7), he knows that his position in the church in Corinth still may not be secure.

Some in the Corinthian church still question his integrity. He had promised to visit them again, and he has not yet done so. "Paul can't be trusted," they said, so now he must defend his word. He writes plainly, he reminds them, "with frankness and godly sincerity" (1:12). He had indeed planned to make them two more visits, coming and going on his way to and from Macedonia. If he let them down about that expected visit, he insists, it was because he was divinely guided (v. 12). Later he explains that if he had come earlier it probably would have stirred up even more trouble.

Want to Know More?

About the pattern of ancient letters? See William M. Ramsay, *The Westminster Guide to the Books of the Bible* (Louisville, Ky.: Westminster John Knox Press, 1994), 396–97.

About words such as *grace, peace, and comfort*? See Geoffrey W. Bromiley, *Theological Dictionary of the New Testament* (Grand Rapids: William B. Eerdmans Publishing Company, 1985).

Since he didn't keep his promise to visit, some accuse Paul of "vacillating," of talking out of both sides of his mouth. They accuse him of saying on the one hand, "Yes, yes," and then turning around and saying, "No, no." Their criticism seems petty. We can be grateful for it, however, for it causes Paul to write a ringing affirmation of the trustworthiness of Christ and of God. To help support that claim to trustworthiness he recalls the ministry of Silvanus (or Silas) and Timothy as well as his own among them (compare Acts 18:5). The Christ they all three preached never spoke double-talk. This leads him to give us one of the great texts of this letter: "For in him every one of God's promises is a 'Yes'" (2 Cor. 1:20).

The Old Testament, to which Paul refers, is a book of promises, many never literally fulfilled: a miraculous temple, restoration of all twelve tribes, and a conquering king. The promised Messiah-King did indeed come, but how much more glorious than even the prophets could dream! His body became that new temple, and not just twelve tribes but all races have become part of his people. "All the [Old Testament's] promises . . . find their Yes in him" (1:20, RSV).

"For this reason . . . we say the 'Amen,' to the glory of God" (1:20). The child in Bil Keane's delightful comic cartoon series *Family Circus* is on her knees, having said her prayers. She explains to her mother that saying "Amen" is like pushing the send button on the e-mail. "Amen," however, is not just a period at the end of the prayer; it is an affirmation. "Amen" is the congregation saying that they are partners with the one who has led the prayer and that we join in affirming that prayer together. "Amen" is an expression of assurance, of faith.

> "'Amen' means 'so be it' or 'let it be so.' It expresses our complete confidence in the triune God, the God of the covenant with Israel as fulfilled through our Lord Jesus Christ, who makes no promise that will not be kept, and whose steadfast love and mercy endures forever."—Question 134, *The Study Catechism, Full Version* (Louisville, Ky.: Geneva Press, 1998), 32.

Some promises to us have not yet been fulfilled, it is true. Later in the letter Paul will write of the promise of life after death. He will affirm of himself and of the Corinthians, however, that God has established God's truth in themselves. They have the seal of the divine notary (1:22). When you buy a house, what guarantees the contract is a seal—a seal and one other thing. You have to make a down payment, earnest money. We have not yet fully received the eternal life God promises us, but we have received the down payment. We have the Holy Spirit. That Spirit assures us that God's word and all God's promises are true. Amen!

? Questions for Reflection

1. What examples can you give of people who were able to help others because they had been through suffering themselves?

2. In what ways are we "partners" with Christ and with each other?
3. "Burnout" is a professional hazard for ministers. Paul is deeply distressed because at one time it seemed that the church at Corinth was not supporting him spiritually and emotionally. In what ways do you and your congregation show your spiritual and emotional support for your pastor? (Your pastor needs it!)
4. Paul affirms the truth of all the scripture's promises. What promises of scripture are your favorites?

2   2 Corinthians 1:23–2:17

Tough Love and Victory

I love Jesus, but I don't even *like* Paul," a woman new to Bible study once confessed to me. There were people in the church at Corinth who did not like Paul either. Paul, however, certainly loved them! No other book in all his writings shows how passionately devoted he was to a congregation that he had founded.

Remains of the Temple of Apollo at Corinth

The Diplomacy of Love (1:23–2:4)

Paul's second visit to Corinth, one not recorded in Acts, had been a disaster. Somebody had stirred up trouble with Paul and upset the whole congregation. Nobody knows just what that person did, but it was devastating to Paul. Now quibblers in the church were criticizing Paul even more for cancelling a return visit. So he begins this section by swearing his explanation. If he had come as originally planned, his presence would have just made things worse (1:23).

Immediately, however, he pulls back to make clear that he doesn't mean that he either would or could have bossed them around. Tactfully he reassures them that he knows that they can stand on their own faith and that he does not want to be their dictator. He seeks to be their fellow worker sharing with them in joyful partnership (v. 24).

The chapter divisions in our Bibles are not inspired. Writing about 2 Corinthians 2:1, John Calvin comments: "Whoever it was that divided the chapters, made a foolish division." The first verses of chapter 2 simply carry on the explanation begun in the first chapter. If Paul had come to them in painful judgment, he explains, they and he would both have been miserable, and, as Calvin puts it, "He cannot feel joyful unless he sees them happy."

So Paul had written a letter, apparently sending it by young Titus. It was so severe that he later wished that he had not sent it. Stern as it was, however, it was sent in love. J. B. Phillips paraphrases verse 4 as "I wrote to you in deep distress and out of a most unhappy heart (I don't mind telling you I shed tears over that letter), not, believe me, to cause you pain, but to show you how deep is my care for your welfare" (Phillips 1957, 73). Calvin comments on this verse, "It is the part of the pious pastor to weep within himself before he calls upon others to weep."

> "Paul's severity derives from his love."— Best, *Second Corinthians*, Interpretation, 20 (Atlanta: John Knox Press, 1987).

"That pastor never takes a stand; he goes along with anything," a friend once commented. Paul took a strict stand. He did not want to. Paul knew, however, that the function of a loving minister is not only to comfort the afflicted but to afflict the comfortable. Paul is like a father I know who had done everything else to try to win his son back to the right path. Finally, in deep distress, he ordered that young man to leave the house, cut off further financial support, and announced that he would no longer try to get him out of his repeated troubles with the law. That "tough love," along with many other expressions of continued affection and much prayer, seems to have helped make a man of that boy. Paul would approve. His letter was to do something like that for the church.

Discipline and Forgiveness (2:5–11)

Apparently Paul's letter helped. Though the offense may have been directed at Paul, the congregation had recognized, as Paul reminds them, that when one suffers all the church suffers (2 Cor. 2:5; compare his words to them in 1 Cor. 12:26). Accordingly, they had "punished" the offender (2 Cor. 2:6). Just what they had done we do not know, but in some way the church had disciplined the troublemaker. The Roman Catholic church requires its members to confess their sins to the priest and to do whatever penance the priest imposes. Minutes of Protestant churches of two hundred years ago show that they often disciplined members for drunkenness, adultery, and other sins. The Corinthian church disciplined this member, the offender repented, and now all seems to be forgiven.

Paul eagerly supports that forgiveness: "Decide in favor of love for him" (as Paul Sampley [2000, 54] translates part of v. 8 in his commentary in the New Interpreter's Bible series, vol. 11). Paul's concern now is for his former enemy, that this person not be overwhelmed—literally, "swallowed up"—by too much sorrow for sin. Paul, their teacher of Christian ethics, had written them to test them, and they had passed the test (v. 9)! Now Paul forgives the offender, too.

Remember that the Corinthians were new Christians. The concept of Christian forgiveness was one they had to be taught. Paul's word for "forgiveness" is used for the canceling of debt, release from prison, or graciously restoring relationship. Forgiveness was not an obligation taught in Corinthian culture. Stoics forbade forgiveness; it violates justice. Psalmists prayed God to forgive them, but no psalmist prayed God to forgive the psalmist's enemies.

> "To err is human; to forgive, divine."—
> Alexander Pope.

Forgiveness still surprises us. In 1988 white supremacist John W. King murdered African American James B. Byrd Jr., chaining him behind his truck and dragging him to death. Four years later King was executed. "I began thinking, 'How can this help me or solve my pain?' And I realized it couldn't," Byrd's son explained (*Newsweek*, July 15, 2002, 17). Young Byrd organized a prayer vigil outside the prison gate. Such Christian forgiveness seems almost as strange to us as it must have to the Corinthians.

"Whom you forgive, I forgive," Paul announces. Indeed, Paul later expressed much of his theology and ethic in these few words: "Be kind to one another, tenderhearted, forgiving one another, as God in Christ has forgiven you" (Eph. 4:32).

"We do this [forgive] so that we may not be outwitted by Satan" (2 Cor. 2:11). Forgiveness is for the sake of the forgiver as well as the one forgiven. To illustrate: The Academy Award–winning film *Dead Man Walking* was based in part on the story of Debbie Morris. She was taken to a remote spot, her boyfriend was murdered, and sixteen-year-old Debbie was raped. David Waters quoted Debbie. in the *Memphis Commercial Appeal* (August 16, 1996) as saying:

> My reluctance to forgive was like a darkness inside, a barrier that barred joy and love. . . . I knew I had to forgive [the rapist-murderer] not for his sake, but for mine. Until I did there was no escaping the hold his evil had on my soul. . . . The only hope for healing—for the people who commit these horrible crimes and for the people who these things happen to—the only hope we have is in God.

Paul would say that Debbie outwitted Satan!

Victory (2:12–14)

Paul returns to his story. He had sent Titus to Corinth, asking for a report. He was so eager to hear that he could not wait, so he went as far as Troas searching for his young assistant. Always preaching everywhere, Paul had found "an open door" in Troas; that is, he found people ready to hear his gospel message. He was so concerned for the beloved church at Corinth, however, that he told Troas good-bye and crossed the narrow sea to Greece, still looking for Titus.

"But thanks be to God[!]" he cries (2 Cor. 2:14). Presumably Paul's Corinthian readers knew what Paul is talking about. The letter itself does not tell us until 7:6, where Paul tells how Titus brought him the good news that all was reconciled in Corinth.

With a cry of thanks Paul proposes a delightful set of figures of speech about who he is but also who his readers are, then and now. To understand the first one, picture a Cecil B. DeMille Hollywood spectacular, only infinitely more colossal. A victorious Roman emperor, coming back after a great battle, would have a parade called a "triumph." The emperor would lead the procession, accompanied by trumpets and drums and marching soldiers, and the captured kings and generals would be dragged in chains to their deaths. Christ, Paul is saying, leads such a victory celebration. We are Christ's captives.

A professor of literature would give Paul an "A" for original imagery but a "D minus" for mixing his metaphors. For though Paul has said we are led as Christ's captives, in the very next verse Paul says

> "Paul never lets the demands for consistency keep him from saying what he considers important."—Floyd V. Filson and James Reid, *The Second Epistle to the Corinthians*, Interpreter's Bible 10, 303.

that we are joyful participants in Christ's victory. Perhaps the late nineteenth-century hymn writer George Matheson best succeeds in capturing Paul's paradoxical figure:

> Make me a captive, Lord.
> Then I shall be free.

You Are God's Perfume (2:14–16)

Mixed in with the other figures is this startling one: We spread the "fragrance" of Christ (v. 14), for we ourselves are "the aroma" of the Lord (v. 15)! This word picture would suggest several things to Paul's readers. In the emperor's triumphal procession there would be not only sights to excite the eyes and music to excite the ears, there would also be incense, spreading that kind of beauty everywhere to celebrate the triumph. (Never mind that he has just said we are the captives in the parade; we are also that incense.) Thus we advertise Christ's Easter victory.

 Want to Know More?

About Titus? Read 2 Corinthians 8:16–24; Galatians 2:1–3; 2 Timothy 4:10; and the epistle that bears Titus's name.

About triumphs? Read the section on 2 Corinthians 2:14 in William Barclay's commentary, *The Letters to the Corinthians*, rev. ed., Daily Bible Study (Louisville, Ky.: Westminster John Knox Press, 2002).

About incense in worship? Check out "incense, worship" on the Web.

The figure also has connotations of the offering of incense as an act of devotion to God. The Old Testament commanded Israel to offer incense. The Corinthian church's former pagans would be familiar with incense offered to gods. Roman Catholic, Orthodox, and "high church" Episcopal churches regularly worship God with incense. Most Protestants use all the other senses: touch as we shake hands, taste with the communion bread, sight with flowers in beautiful churches, and hearing with our music. Many of us, however, have to think ourselves back into the first century to grasp Paul's figure about ourselves as incense. Paul is saying that just as incense is offered to God, so we ourselves are to be offered to our Lord and Savior (compare Rom. 12:1).

Our Awesome Responsibility (2:15–17)

Paul extracts one more meaning from his use of the figure of incense. When Romans smelled the incense of the emperor's triumphal parade they rejoiced in victory. For the vanquished, however, it was the aroma that they smelled on their way to their death.

Paul never speaks of some middle ground. There are those whose response to the gospel is to take the grim road from death to death. It is a process going on, and it may be that those who witness to them can help turn them in the other direction. Still, Paul can speak of some people as in the process of perishing, even as others are moving upward from life to life.

Jesus, too, warned of the awesome responsibility placed upon us. "Whatever you bind on earth will be bound in heaven, and whatever you loose on earth will be loosed in heaven" (Matt. 18:18).

If that responsibility seems too big for us, join Paul! "Who is sufficient for these things?" he cries. Who is competent to take on such awesome responsibility? In one's own strength, nobody. Read Paul's fuller answer to that question in 2 Corinthians 3:4–5. At this point he pauses to say who is *not* competent to serve as Christ's incense. It is those whom he calls "peddlers of God's word" (2:17).

Ancient Greece was familiar with traveling teachers. In his *Protagoras*, Plato pictures Socrates as making fun of a teacher of ethics who has arrived in Athens offering prospective students a money-back guarantee. "If after taking my course," the false teacher was promising in effect, "you don't feel you are a good person, then I will return your money." Such a charlatan could not lose! Calvin says that the word Paul uses for these who "peddle" Christianity is related to innkeepers who secretly adulterate what they then sell as fine wine.

> "It is not true that love is blind. It has penetrating insight into moral reality."—Floyd V. Filson and James Reid, *The Second Epistle to the Corinthians*, Interpreter's Bible 10, 295.

The big thing wrong with Corinth's false teachers, however, is not that they may be teaching an adulterated gospel; it is that they are doing it for money. Kierkegaard is quoted as saying that the most subtle trick of Satan is to get people to do the right thing from the wrong motive. It may be that some of our television evangelists have been what Paul would call "peddlers of the gospel." Perhaps some of us have wrong motivations in the good things we do, too.

Paul speaks of himself as a Christian minister, but all through this letter he is careful to include the laypeople of the Corinthian church as partners. How, then, can we all assume the awesome responsibility of spreading the gospel? Paul ends the chapter by giving us three hints (2:17). We must do so with sincerity. We must do so remembering that we are "persons sent from God"—that is, in our own way, we are apostles. Finally, we do so always "standing in his presence" (literally, "standing before [God's] face"). Remember, a loving God sees us sincerely trying. That may give us courage even when only God can see good results.

? Questions for Reflection

1. In what ways would you like your pastor to "comfort the afflicted," and in what ways would you really like your pastor to "afflict" us who are "comfortable"?
2. The Corinthian church disciplined an offender. In what ways, if any, should your church discipline its members?
3. In how many different ways that you can think of is the life of a true Christian like "perfume," incense for Christ?
4. You have now studied the first two chapters of 2 Corinthians. So far, which ideas in them have interested you most and meant most to you?

3

Our Mission and Our Glory

This chapter contains delightful figures, promises of life and liberty, and such strange exegesis of such obscure Old Testament passages that one is tempted to skip half of it. Don't! If you dig a bit you may discover in it a glory so brilliant that it offers transforming life and freedom.

You Are a Letter of Christ (3:1–4)

It begins with imaginative figures of speech. The newcomers to Corinth who were undermining Paul's work and reputation had arrived with letters of recommendation. Paul laughs at the thought that he might need such testimonials from others (3:1). You yourselves are our letter of recommendation, he says lovingly. Look around you at your fellow church members, your brothers and sisters in your congregation that I helped start. What more recommendation could anyone ask for!

Now comes a delightful metaphor: "You are a letter of Christ" (3:3). Us? Yes. In the Greek, the word "you" is emphatic, as though Paul had written, "*You* are a letter of Christ." Paul is the instrument, but Christ is the writer. One should never press a parable or a metaphor too far, but it would not be utterly beyond Paul's figure to make this comparison: Christ is the writer; Paul is the pen; the Holy Spirit is the ink; the hearts of us Christians are the paper; and all those around us are the readers, for we are "known and read by all" (v. 2).

That phrase about others "reading us" is sobering. Paul Gilbert put the challenge like this:

You are writing a Gospel
A chapter each day,
By deeds that you do,
By words that you say.
Men read what you write,
Whether faithless or true;
Say, what is the Gospel
According to you?

Actually Christ, not we, does the writing, but as our hearts are open to the Holy Spirit—and only then—we grow to become genuine letters from our Lord to those around us.

We Are Ministers of the New Covenant (3:4–6)

The Christians at Corinth are Paul's proof that the attacks on him are not valid. Quickly, however, he humbly affirms that his ministry's effectiveness is not because he himself is such a great preacher and pastor. He can claim no competence for himself. He is only, as Calvin puts it, a "channel" for the Spirit. Yet now in that sense he can answer the cry of awe that he has just voiced a few verses earlier: "Who is sufficient for these things?" (2:16). Humble as he is, Paul can claim that he himself is "sufficient," competent, and so are we, because "our competence is from God, who has made us competent to be ministers of a new covenant" (3:5–6). In different ways we have been called by God to that task of ministry. Our assurance that we can do it comes from the power of the Holy Spirit, bestowed on us in that new covenant. That new covenant "is not of letter but of spirit" (v. 6). What Paul means by that new covenant will be the subject of the rest of the chapter.

> "If we are to live, life must come not from some code of behavior but from God; thus it is the Spirit that 'gives life.'"—Best, *Second Corinthians*, Interpretation, 29–30.

Our Bible is divided into Old Testament (or Covenant, a different translation of the same word) and the New Testament (or Covenant). God rescued Israel from slavery and gave them a law code, carved in stone. They failed to keep that covenant. Yet, as Jerusalem was about to be destroyed, the prophet Jeremiah dreamed, "The days are surely coming . . . when I will make a new covenant with the house of Israel. . . . But this is the covenant that I will make . . . : I will put my law within them, and I will write it on their hearts" (Jer. 31:31–33;

compare 2 Cor. 3:3). Down through the centuries, the people never quite lost that hope. At the last supper, Jesus announced to his disciples, "This cup is the new covenant in my blood" (1 Cor. 11:25). What God's people had longed for had come at last!

This new covenant would be a covenant not of word (or of "written code," RSV) but of the Spirit: "not of letter but of spirit; for the letter kills, but the Spirit gives life" (2 Cor. 3:6). Laws, even God-given laws, do not empower people. Paul means more than simply that "Love God" and "Love your neighbor" give the "spirit" of the law. Even that command to love is still a command, and in the end, by itself, it leads to the frustrating realization that we have failed. Rather, the new covenant is one in which the Holy Spirit writes on our hearts. That Spirit can change people; the Spirit "gives life."

Barclay comments that there are two words in Greek for "new." One means simply new in time, but the other means new in kind. The *new* covenant is not just one that came at a later calendar date; it is a covenant utterly new and different, so "much more" than the old.

The New Testament Is More Glorious Even than the Old (3:7–13)

Up to this point in this chapter Paul has been writing in a balanced series of contrasts: *not* with ink *but* with the Spirit, *not* on stone *but* on hearts, *not* competence from ourselves *but* from God, and so on. One way to get Paul's message is to see how many such contrasts you can find and what they add up to. Now, however, Paul describes a different sort of contrast. See how many ways you can find just in verses 7–11 that Paul says *how much more* the New Testament has going for it than did even the Old.

Behind these verses lies a story. It was familiar to Paul's readers who knew the Jewish scriptures, but we may need to be reminded. Exodus 34:29–33 tells us that when Moses came down from Mount Sinai, bearing the stone tables of the Ten Commandments, his face shone with glory. He had been in the presence of the glorious God. Indeed his face was so aglow with glory that he began to wear a veil so as not to blind the eyes of the people who saw and heard him. Paul affirms the great glory of the old covenant. But how much more glorious is the new! Paul says it offers not condemnation but justification (compare Rom. 3:21–25).

A modern Old Testament professor might give Paul an "F" at certain points on his interpretation of the Jewish scriptures, but rabbis of his day would understand. Paul goes beyond what Exodus actually says to affirm that in a few days the glory faded from Moses' face as a suntan fades when you leave the beach. This may be hinted at in Exodus and was perhaps tradition in Paul's day. The fading of God's glory from Moses' face Paul takes as symbolic. The Old Testament was glorious, but it is fading away; the New is eternal (2 Cor. 3:11–13).

He explains the greater glory of the New Testament by an implied metaphor of this modern kind: Each night at the airport a huge electric searchlight is bright indeed, but compared to the light of the sun next morning it fades almost into nothing. In the same way "what once had glory [the old covenant] has lost its glory because of the greater glory [of the new]" (3:10).

Only Christ Enables Us Fully to See That Glory (3:14–15)

Now Paul really does go far beyond what Exodus actually says. He turns that story around backward to make his point. He takes that veil off Moses' face and puts it over the faces of the Israelites. That veil causes them to fail to see God's glory that the New Covenant brings. He says that those who have rejected Christ have had "their minds [one could also translate this "hearts"] . . . hardened" (3:14). They hear God's word read every week in the synagogue, but they fail to see how all its promises find their *yes* in Christ (1:20). It is through Christ that the scripture can be rightly understood (3:15–16).

"It is impossible to overstate the importance of the Holy Spirit for Paul's understanding of the life of faith."—J. Paul Sampley, *The Second Letter to the Corinthians*, New Interpreter's Bible 11 (Nashville: Abingdon Press, 2000), 73.

Paul is grieving over his fellow Jews who have rejected Jesus. Surely Christians should share the gospel with Jews as best we can. It may be more important for our immediate purposes, however, to consider how important it is for us ourselves to understand the scripture always through Christ. Some years ago Bill Moyers led a series of discussions of Genesis on public television. The night they discussed Noah and the flood he asked a reporter on the panel, "How would you word a headline for that story?" "*Angry God Destroys Humankind,*" he replied, in effect. Peter Gomes, an older African American pastor, responded gently, "I'd have said, '*God Gives Humankind Another Chance*.'" He read it in the light of Christ! So must we. Frequently the Old Testament and the New have been used to condone war, slavery, and the subordination of women. Certainly the "letter" of the Bible does say such things. "But when one turns to the Lord, the veil is removed," Paul says (3:6). Christians are always to read the Bible in the glorious light of Jesus Christ, taking as our authority what, even in stories of violence and outdated rules, points to him. Treating the Bible as a written code, a rule book, kills; reinterpreting it to find something in every passage witnessing to God's love gives life.

A Vision of That Glory Transforms Us (3:16–18)

Behind the last verses of this chapter lies an idea familiar to all educated Greeks in Corinth. In the *Republic* and the *Symposium* Plato had proposed that the soul of the truly wise may be lifted to a "beatific vision" of absolute beauty and truth—in a sense, of God. When that happens, the soul will never again be quite the same. Far better than Plato, Paul knows where such a transforming vision may be found. It is in "seeing the glory of the Lord" (3:18).

When Christ takes off the veil of the old "written code," Christ sets us free (3:16). In his treatise on Christian liberty, Martin Luther describes the paradox of Christian freedom in two sentences:

> "The best teacher on earth cannot teach the man who knows it all already and who does not wish to learn. God gave us free will, and, if we insist upon our own way, we cannot learn [God's will]."—William Barclay, *The Letters to the Corinthians*, rev. ed., Daily Study Bible (Louisville, Ky.: Westminster John Knox Press, 2002).

A Christian is a perfectly free lord of all, subject to none.
A Christian is a perfectly dutiful servant of all, subject to all.

Christ gives the freedom that he himself demonstrated when he came as the Servant of all.

When the veil is removed, what we see is reflected glory, God's glory reflected as in a mirror from the face of Jesus Christ. Behind that image is a story so strange that it seems to modern readers almost weird. We are told that Moses begged to see God in all the divine glory. The glory of God's face, however, was too brilliant for even

Moses to see directly. So God let Moses hide behind some rocks and passed by, allowing Moses to see God's back (Exod. 33:17–23). Now, however, even we can see the glory of the Lord "as though reflected as in a mirror" (2 Cor. 3:18). If you want to see God, Paul implies, look at Jesus. See him healing the sick, giving sight to the blind, teaching the Sermon on the Mount, and, most especially, giving his life for you on the cross. There, as in a mirror, you see the glory of God.

The result: We will become like him! We are being "transformed . . . from one degree of glory to another" until we are in his image (3:18). The transformation is not sudden, and in this life it is never complete. The change is by degrees, with ups and downs. Our vision of Christ is still veiled by our sin, but growth does occur. Sometimes when a loving couple have lived together for many years they become so much alike that they even begin to seem to look alike. We have this glorious promise of the end: "Beloved, we are God's children now; what we will be has not yet been revealed. What we do know is this: when he is revealed, we will be like him, for we will see him as he is" (1 John 3:2).

Christ is the mirror, the image of God. Most commentators and translators agree that that is what Paul means—but the Jerusalem Bible translates 2 Corinthians 3:18 as making *us* mirrors of that glory. Perhaps you have been privileged to see a reflection of Christ's glory in the face, or in the life, of some saint you know.

Want to Know More?

About Paul's use of the Old Testament? See Ernest Best, *Second Corinthians,* Interpretation (Atlanta: John Knox Press, 1987), 35–36.

About how we "veil" our eyes when we read the Bible? Read the section on 2 Corinthians 3:12–18 in William Barclay's commentary, *The Letters to the Corinthians,* rev. ed., Daily Bible Study (Louisville, Ky.: Westminster John Knox Press, 2002).

? Questions for Reflection

1. Insofar as it is open to the Holy Spirit, your church is a "letter of Christ." What do people around your church see and "read" in the "letter" that is your congregation?

2. How many times, and in how many ways, can you find the word "Spirit" (or "spirit") used in 2 Corinthians 3? What do these verses teach us about the Holy Spirit?

3. What examples can you give of Old Testament stories and passages—and, for that matter, New Testament ones, too—that take on new and better meaning when they are interpreted in the light of Jesus Christ, the incarnation of God's love?
4. Few of us Christians feel totally "freed." What kind of freedom, then, does the Spirit really bring?

4 2 Corinthians 4:1-18

The Christian's Courage

"**W**e do not lose heart" (2 Cor. 4:1). So Paul begins this chapter. When he gets near the end of the chapter, he sums up what he has written by saying it again: "We do not lose heart" (v. 16). Paul knows that we do at least get "perplexed," and when he says that we get "struck down" (vv. 8–9), he doesn't just mean physically—though that happened to Paul too! A better translation might be: "We don't *keep on being* discouraged" (emphasis added). The Christian's hope restores our courage, even if sometimes we falter.

This chapter will tell us something of what this courage of a Christian means, and why, no matter how hopeless things sometimes seem, we don't continue to lose heart.

We Have the Example of Paul's Courage
(4:1–6)

One thing that must have been discouraging to Paul was that his rivals back in Corinth kept trying to discredit him. He has to try to refute three charges.

The first is that he is using clever techniques, tricks that perhaps get a hearing but pervert the truth of the gospel. He replies by simply reminding them of what they really know: Paul always "told it like it is." His was a "let-the-chips-fall-where-they-may" kind of preaching, "the open statement of the truth" (4:2). So, Corinthians, he says in effect, let your "conscience" be your guide (v. 2). There are clever preachers in pulpits or perhaps even on television who say only what people want to hear and draw great crowds. Not Paul!

Paul's lack of universal popularity leads to another criticism, though: Paul failed, his rivals grumble, with so many people. Paul's answer is "In their case the god of this world [or age] has blinded" their minds (4:4). Paul would never allow those who have rejected Christ to make the delightful excuse popularized by the comedian Flip Wilson, whose character Geraldine hilariously justified anything she did by saying, "The devil made me do it!" Sometimes the biblical book of Exodus says that God hardened Pharaoh's heart, and sometimes it says that Pharaoh hardened his heart himself. The problem of evil has no simple solution. For Paul, though, Satan is real and active and leads forces of evil against those of the Lord. There is real, cosmic evil in the world. In an era when people think that "anything goes" and that the only unforgivable sin is intolerance, we hear few sermons about Satan. The wanton destruction of the World Trade Center on September 11, 2001, dramatized the fact that some acts really are satanic. So far as we can tell, it is simply fact that there are those "who are perishing," "blinded . . . [to] the light of the gospel of the glory of Christ" (2 Cor. 4:3, 4). Heaven knows, Paul tried to reach them.

There is one more implied charge, that, as Paul puts it, we "proclaim ourselves"—in other words, that Paul seeks glory for himself. Paul's answer is shocking. He says that what he wants to be is not somebody the Corinthians are to look up to; he wants to be their *slave* (4:5). The New Testament often uses other words for "servant," but Paul uses the most blunt one, "slave." Jesus used that word, too (Matt. 20:27).

We Are Only Clay Pots, but We Carry Treasure (4:7–12)

Paul does like vivid figures of speech! We are only clay pots, but "we have this treasure in clay jars" (2 Cor. 4:7). The treasure is "the light of the knowledge of the glory of God in the face of Jesus Christ" (v. 6). God uses even us clay vessels to carry that knowledge to the world.

Behind these verses is a story Paul's readers knew, the story of creation. God's first words in the

Paul used the image of clay pots to describe the human body.

Bible are "Let there be light" (Gen. 1:3; compare 2 Cor. 4:6). Now that light "has shone in our hearts" (2 Cor. 4:6). At the climax of the creation story God said, "Let us make humankind in our image, according to our likeness" (Gen. 1:26). "God formed man from the dust of the ground" (Gen. 2:7), the same material as the other animals. Yet though made of clay, Adam and Eve were in the image of God. Sin, however, corrupted that image. Now with Christ that image appears again in all its glory. Little by little we are being transformed inwardly again into that image (2 Cor. 3:18). We are still clay, but there is something glorious within us.

> "We tend to glorify biblical characters. . . . We surmise that they . . . have no doubt, that they do not struggle as we do. But note well that Paul describes himself . . . as being near the brink of what he can bear, as about to fall over the edge. . . . As downtrodden and crushed as Paul was, however, he was convinced that God would never let him go."—J. Paul Sampley, *The Second Letter to the Corinthians*, New Interpreter's Bible 11, 88.

Paul likes to set one thing over against another. One good way to study 4:7–12 is to see how many contrasts you can find in just these five verses. Verses 8 and 9 list some of these difficulties Paul has gone through. Some of us have experienced troubles, too! Paul's main point here is not to describe what he has endured as signs of his faithfulness, though he will do that later (11:23–29). His point is to illustrate how weak and frail this earthen pot is: afflicted, crushed, perplexed, knocked down. Yet there is treasure even in such fragile vessels. That enables Paul—and us—to keep going. It is not through our own strength but God's.

By the time Paul wrote this letter he must have been an ugly sight. After all those beatings his back was bound to be a swollen mass of scar tissue, and that stoning he endured at Lystra had not improved his face. After so many broken bones he must have been crippled with arthritis. Once, in fact, he had been mistaken for a corpse (Acts 14:19)! Given his "outer nature," he would not have made it as a star on television. He described himself as "carrying in the body the death of Jesus." There is a lovely legend that that most saintly of saints, Francis of Assisi, lived such a Christ-like life that eventually he received in his body the *stigmata*, Christ's wounds in his hands, feet, and side. People could see in Paul's broken body a symbol of Christ's death, too (2 Cor. 4:10).

Paul loves paradoxes. Precisely as the sufferings and death of Christ are manifested in his frail body, there the life of Christ can shine through, too (4:11). Sometimes we, too, get a glimpse of Christ's glory as we see people who have gone through suffering for the sake of their Lord.

Thus We Can Speak and Act with Courage
(4:13–15)

Behind these verses lies another story. In Psalm 116, the psalmist tells how he had suffered and nearly died. He had endured not only physical illness but also difficulties inflicted by liars. God has restored him, though, and he testifies thankfully that

> I kept my faith, even when I said,
> "I am greatly afflicted."
>
> Ps. 116:10

Paul had kept the faith even when afflicted, and he too had borne testimony. Quoting another version of Psalm 116:10, he writes, "I believed, and so I spoke" (2 Cor. 4:13). So it is with all who are faithful. One thinks of white ministers in the South in the 1960s who lost their beloved churches when they spoke out for civil rights, and, even more, of those courageous African Americans who risked much more for freedom. You can name whistle-blowers and other heroes and heroines who spoke the truth, no matter what it might cost.

> "'Our outer nature' is the life we live among other people in which we may be persecuted or suffer in other ways (see 4:8–11). 'Our inner nature' is the new life that comes into being with our relationship to Christ when we become new beings (5:17)."—Best, *Second Corinthians*, Interpretation, 45.

What gives that courage is the knowledge that "the one who raised the Lord Jesus will raise us also" (4:14). On the great day at the end of time we will be brought into his presence. As we testify now to this "amazing grace" more and more people are won to Christ, and all "overflows," as Calvin says in reference to verse 15, "in thanksgiving to the glory of God."

Our Courage Is Based on Christian Realism
(4:16–18)

Paul began this chapter saying that "we do not lose heart," that though we have our ups and downs we don't continue in discouragement. Now he begins the last paragraph of this chapter, "So we do not lose heart" (4:16). Some readers of this book are very much aware that "our outer nature is wasting away" (v. 16). Yet sometimes even in invalids, even in people who are close to death, we can see God's glory shining through, for their "inner nature is being renewed day by day" (v. 16). Thinking of the eternal, they don't "lose heart."

The "eternal weight of glory" (v. 17) is a curious phrase. Though the Old Testament word for *glory* does have connotations of weight, glory is usually symbolized by light, and light does not weigh very much. Yet Paul imagines a pair of scales. On one side are the afflictions that we go through as we try now to live as Christians in this life. He has admitted that sometimes those afflictions have been so heavy that they have crushed him. On the other side of the scales is the infinite glory of eternal life to come. Weighed in that balance, those crushing troubles seem less than feather weight. A computer language is named for the great mathematician Pascal. He said that the Christian bets only a life of perhaps seventy years in the hope of winning life that goes on forever. The odds are one to infinity. Who could turn down odds like that!

> "But if we have the Christian view, the sufferings of earth will be no more than the chisel strokes of the sculptor, forgotten in the beauty of the statue which he is shaping from the marble, or even welcomed as the means of his achievement. The lost pleasures of life, the things that are denied us, will be no more than the fragments that are chipped from the stone to liberate the artistic masterpiece."—Floyd V. Filson and James Reid, *The Second Epistle to the Corinthians*, Interpreter's Bible 10, 324.

Paul ends with the kind of "realism" that would be familiar to his Greek readers who knew Plato's philosophy. Plato distinguished the real from the unreal by its permanence. I dream of a million dollars, but when I wake up it vanishes; it is not real. Real things endure. Material things, "what can be seen," decay and end; true realities, spiritual realities, "what cannot be seen," are forever (4:18). Paul knows that truth. Christians live for what is really, eternally real.

That leads directly into Paul's further assurance of the glorious life to come, in our "house not made with hands, eternal in the heavens," but that is the subject of the next chapter.

? Questions for Reflection

1. What in the Christian faith gives you courage as you face the troubles of life?
2. What examples can you give of people who spoke out boldly for the truth, even when it might cost them to do so?

3. "We have this treasure in earthen vessels" is a delightful figure full of all kinds of meaning. What things does that figure say to you?

4. Make a list, even chart them out to look at, of all the contrasts Paul describes in this chapter. What meanings do they add up to?

Want to Know More?

About the word *glory*? See Easton's Bible dictionary on the Web at www.ccel.org/e/easton/ebd/ebd.html, or other Bible dictionaries.

About sufferings Paul endured? See 2 Corinthians 11:23–33 and Acts 13–28.

About Plato's view of genuine reality? See Plato's "Allegory of the Cave" on the Web.

5 2 Corinthians 5:1-21

Ambassadors Far from Home

In 2 Corinthians 4, Paul introduced the subject of realities that we do not see. One of these, enormously important to all of us, is a reality we cannot yet see, but he assures us that we will see it some day. It is our future life, and 2 Corinthians 5 gives us some pictures to describe it.

We Have a Home Away from Home (5:1-5)

The body you live in now, Paul says, is like a tent. It can and will be folded up and destroyed. We have a permanent house in heaven, though, of which God is the architect and builder (2 Cor. 5:1; compare John 14:2). Sometimes, as Paul well knew, the burdens of this life are so heavy that we groan for that other life. It is not that we want to die (to be "found naked," 2 Cor. 5:3), but we may long for heaven. Paul does not mind mixing his metaphors; now he compares this mortal body to a ragged suit. He yearns for Christ to cover him with a finer, eternal garment. In *The Letters to the Corinthians*, Barclay explains Paul's meaning in this verse by saying, "It is not so much that we desire to be stripped of this house, but rather that we desire to put on our heavenly body over it." Paul was still hoping that

"Someday you will read in the papers that D. L. Moody, of East Northfield, is dead. Don't you believe a word of it. At that moment I shall be more alive than I am now. I shall have gone up higher, that is all—out of this old clay tenement into a house that is immortal, a body that death cannot touch, that sin cannot taint, a body fashioned like his glorious body."—Evangelist Dwight L. Moody, as quoted in *Senior Bible Studies*, October–December, 1961, by Dr. and Mrs. William M. Ramsay (Richmond: Presbyterian Church in the United States, 1961), 10.

Christ would come again in his lifetime and that he would never die, but also that his present life would be "swallowed up"—to get in another metaphor (!)—by the life to come (v. 4).

Benjamin Franklin was not a great theologian, but he wrote for himself an epitaph not entirely unlike Paul's figures of speech:

> The body of
> B. Franklin, Printer
> (Like the Cover of an Old Book
> Its contents torn Out
> And Stript of its Lettering and Gilding)
> Lies Here, Food for Worms.
> But the Work shall not be Lost;
> For it will (as he Believ'd) Appear once More
> In a New and More Elegant Edition
> Revised and Corrected
> By the Author.

Best is right that it is useless to try to figure out exactly what Paul thought about the state of Christians between their death and the return of the Lord. Paul assured the Thessalonians that those who had already died were not going to miss out on the great day of the Lord (1 Thess. 4:13–18), and John sees the souls of martyrs already in heaven (Rev. 6:9). In his discussion of 2 Corinthians 5:1–6, Calvin attempts to put together the idea that at death we go straight to heaven and yet at the second coming we are raised from the dead. He writes of our "house": "The blessed condition of the soul after death is the commencement of this building, but the glory of the final resurrection is the consummation of it."

How do we know that the promise of that future "house" is true? We already have the down payment on it, the Holy Spirit (5:5)!

We Live Now Aware of That Future Home (5:6–12)

With that assurance "we are always confident" (5:7), even though we live now with a tension between two worlds. Our grandparents used to sing "This World Is Not My Home." The late Burl Ives taught many to sing an 1800s folk hymn:

> I'm just a poor, wayfaring stranger,
> Traveling through this world of woe.

But there's no sickness, toil or danger,
   In that fair land, to which I go,
I'm going home . . .
I'm going home.

Later in his life, when Paul was a prisoner facing execution, he wrote, "I am hard pressed between the two: my desire is to depart and be with Christ, for that is far better; but to remain in the flesh is more necessary for you" (Phil. 1:23–24). Here he says much the same thing: "We would rather be away from the body and at home with the Lord" (2 Cor. 5:8). Assured by the Spirit, however, even here we can "walk [live] by faith, not by sight," by Christ-given hope, not by the things of this world that our earthbound eyes see around us (v. 7). So we must keep on serving.

Want to Know More?

About the Christian hope? See Shirley C. Guthrie Jr., *Christian Doctrine,* rev. ed. (Louisville, Ky.: Westminster John Knox Press, 1994), chapter 19; John H. Leith, *Basic Christian Doctrine* (Louisville, Ky.: Westminster/John Knox Press, 1993), chapter 22; *The Study Catechism* (Louisville, Ky.: Geneva Press, 1998), questions 85–88.

Right now what matters for Christ's people is not whether we continue to live in this home or go on to our heavenly home; it is that we "aim to please him" (5:9). "For all of us must appear before the judgment seat of Christ" (v. 10). That is, our assurance for life to come is no excuse for neglecting our responsibilities in this life now. Sometimes the church has made the mistake of presenting the gospel as a way we can get into heaven while ignoring our responsibility toward people all around us. We have a responsibility toward those who are poor and sick, and as Christ's "ambassadors" (v. 20), we must work for peace, not war.

The beautiful words of 2 Corinthians 4:16–5:10 are often read at funerals to comfort us in bereavement. Properly so! We should remember, however, that Paul wrote them to encourage us to live in service to Christ through serving others here and now.

Paul's Present Life Is to Be Judged Not by Appearance but by Service (5:11–15)

Paul's critics in Corinth have tried to distort his image in the minds of that church. Paul replies that he is not going to waste time "commending ourselves to you again" (5:12). Whatever they see, God sees that he is hard at work preaching the gospel (v. 11). He does want them, however, not to be ashamed of the one who had started their church, however he may have been made to appear (v. 12). "So they have said I'm crazy," he says in effect. "Crazy or sane, what I have done has been for you" (v. 13, paraphrased). Perhaps the charge of insanity was based on the fact that Paul did have visions and did speak with tongues. Perhaps it was simply that he was so completely dedicated to his mission that he seemed to some people to be an insane fanatic. Jesus had been called crazy, too (Mark 3:21). Paul was completely dedicated to serving.

> "Human judgments are not merely inadequate. They are also tinged with prejudice and bias. We make them with our own interests in mind. Since Paul's conversion and in the light of his conviction that Christ died for him, he thinks in a different kind of way, once 'according to the flesh' but now 'according to the Spirit.'"—Best, *Second Corinthians,* Interpretation, 53.

The explanation of his behavior is that Christ's love for him "urges [him] on" (2 Cor. 5:14). That word implies at the same time the powerful force of that love's motivation and the narrow limits it sets on his life. It "constrains" him (KJV).

J. B. Phillips paraphrases the difficult verses 14b–15 as saying, "We look at it like this: if One died for all men then, in a sense, they all died, and His purpose in dying for them is that their lives now should be no longer lived for themselves but for Him Who died and rose again for them" (Phillips 1957, 77–78). With that resurrection everything is changed.

We Are Ambassadors Wearing Spectacles (5:16–21)

Because of Christ's death and resurrection, "everything old has passed away; see, everything has become new!" (5:17). Paul's Corinthian readers must have found those words of Paul startling, even incredible. We find them hard to believe, too! The world certainly doesn't *look* new. One great point Paul has been making, though, is that what ordinary eyes see—that is, appearances—are not necessarily things as they really are. True, the new heaven and the new earth will not be manifest fully until the end of time (Rev. 21:1), but we can at least begin to see realities we missed before. Calvin says that looking at the world through the gospel is like putting on a pair of spectacles. For example, Christians now see people in a different way. I go through the checkout line and too often see the cashier much as I do the cash register and the shopping cart—but I know a Christian who sees that cashier differently, as a person, a potential friend, learns her name, and does not look at her "from a human point of view." Paul confesses that in the days before his conversion he had seen even Christ "from a human point of view" (2 Cor. 5:16), but no longer! Christians may begin to see slums not simply as places to be bypassed quickly but as full of people for whom Christ died.

Christians' eyes may see the beauty of all nature in new ways, glimpses of the new earth to come. That is because Christians have been "born again," for "if anyone is in Christ, there is a new creation" (v. 17). You have seen how becoming a Christian can so change a person that seeing that person you get a glimpse of the new creation.

This change is the result of God's "reconciling" us to God's self. Note that here it is not that God has to be reconciled to us; we are the ones who need to be changed. The *Confession of 1967* of the (now) Presbyterian Church (U.S.A.) describes "reconciliation" like this:

Christians see the world through the lens of the gospel.

God's reconciling act in Jesus Christ is a mystery which the Scripture describes in various ways. It is called the sacrifice of a lamb, a shepherd's life given for his sheep, atonement by a priest; again it is ransom of a slave, payment of debt, vicarious satisfaction of a legal penalty, and victory over the powers of evil. These are expressions of a truth which remains beyond the reach of all theory in the depths of God's love for man. They reveal the gravity, cost, and sure achievement of God's reconciling work. (*Book of Confessions*, 9:09)

Paul's figure for reconciliation in verse 19 is that of God, as it were, hitting the delete button on the computer where our sins have been counted.

So, with another of Paul's delightful figures of speech, he says that we are called to be "ambassadors." The function of an ambassador is to promote peace and reconciliation. Barclay compares us to Roman "legates" who might draw up treaties and establish government in some country newly taken over by Rome. We are ambassadors for the conquering Ruler of the universe, seeking to win people to the joyful peace that Ruler can bring.

In my youth we used to sing a hymn based on verses 19 and 20:

I am a stranger here, within a foreign land;
My home is far away, upon a golden strand;
Ambassador to be of realms beyond the sea,
I'm here on business for my king.
This is the message that I bring, a message angels fain would sing:
"Oh, be ye reconciled," Thus saith my Lord and King,
"Oh be ye reconciled to God."

Dr. E. T. Cassel, "The King's Business," as found in *Premier Hymns* (Richmond: Presbyterian Committee on Publication, 1925), #42.

Paul would like that song.

Paul ends the chapter with a mystery that I am sure not even he would claim to understand. On the cross Christ so identified himself with human sin that somehow he *became* sin itself, receiving upon himself the just wrath that a righteous God must feel toward sin. The result: that bunch of sinners in Corinth became "the righteousness of God" (5:21). And so, somehow, in Christ, do we!

"For as persons who are old, or whose eyes are by any means become dim . . . can scarcely read two words together, yet, by the assistance of spectacles, will begin to read distinctly,—so the Scripture . . . dispels the darkness, and gives us a clear view of the true God."—John Calvin, *Institutes of the Christian Religion* (Philadelphia: Presbyterian Board of Christian Education, n.d.), 1.6.

? Questions for Reflection

1. Go ahead, let your imagination take over. What do you look forward to doing and seeing when you reach your heavenly home?
2. In the discussion of reconciliation quoted from the *Confession of 1967,* which pictures mean the most to you? Why?
3. What examples can you give of how the world seems new and different when we are most truly "in Christ"?
4. Go through 2 Corinthians 5. See how many figures of speech, word pictures, you can find. Which are the most meaningful to you? Which are the least meaningful, so that you need to study them more?

2 Corinthians 6:1–7:16

Portrait of a Passionate Pastor

Jesus was "a man of sorrows and acquainted with grief" (Isa. 53:3, KJV). So was Paul! In the minds of many of us a hero is supposed to be a Stoic, a figure like movie star John Wayne, cool, never flinching, unafraid though facing death. Not Paul! Read through 2 Corinthians 6–7 and see how many emotions you can find stated or implied: pride, discouragement, sleepless nights, sorrow, fear, and love are some. "Sometimes," said an ancient report, Paul "looked like a man," very human indeed. Yet, at the end of chapter 7, there is also consolation that comes with the joy of shared reconciliation.

There are times when your own pastor identifies with Paul. Burnout is the occupational hazard of the ministry. Perhaps we ourselves can learn to identify with Paul's congregation at Corinth, where, 2 Corinthians 7 seems to say, dissension was at last replaced by repentance and love.

The Urgency of Our Mission (6:1–2)

Paul has summoned the congregation to a mission: We are to be "ambassadors for Christ." We are to spread the good news that reconciliation has been made possible, and we are to plead with people to join in it. Now Paul seeks to inspire in us that sense of urgency that drove him on. "*Now* is the acceptable time; see, *now* is the day of salvation!" (6:2; italics added).

Jesus had that same kind of drive, never staying long in one place but rushing on, and telling his disciples to move on quickly, to get the gospel word out while there was still time. Paul feels urgency in part because he expected the end of the world in his own day, though he is careful to say that we don't really know when the end will be (1 Thess. 4:13–5:6). In our own day we see the evangelistic zeal of such groups as Jehovah's Witnesses and various Adventist churches. They are sure the end is at hand, so they are willing to go from house to house to spread their message while there is still time.

Once my own denomination had more missionary zeal. Now we no longer sing Mary A. Thompson's words:

Behold how many thousands still are lying
   Bound in the darksome prison house of sin,
With none to tell them of the Savior's dying,
   Or of the life he died for them to win.

People are still dying, however, an estimated 51 million people each year, most of them never having really gotten to know the good news. Each year 11 million mothers watch their young children die. Paul said to his fellow "ambassadors" that *now* is the time for mission.

Most translations miss the ambiguity in 2 Corinthians 6:1. Paul wrote, "As we work together." Most English versions have added "with him," to make it that Paul is saying he works with God. Leave out "with him," and Paul is saying also that church members are to work together with their pastor and with each other as ambassadors of reconciliation.

Paul's Plea as Pastor and Parent (6:3–13)

Roman Catholics call their pastors "Father." Paul might like that. He calls those often straying church members his "children" (6:13). He describes how he has loved them, and he pleads in turn, "Open wide your hearts also" (v. 13).

He reviews his fatherly work for them. Negatively, contrary to what has been charged, he has put no obstacles in anyone's way (6:3). Positively he has gone through for them all the things that he describes in 6:4–10. Paul is the original "survivor." For understanding all that list of things, the key word is "endurance" ("steadfastness," "constancy"). He has never let them down.

True, he has "spoken frankly" to them. Sometimes the truth hurts. As the next chapter explains, one letter he had written them had caused them pain (7:8), but even in that letter he had written because his heart was open to them (6:11). Sometimes, many of us know, parents have to be stern with their children! So a loving pastor must at times warn a congregation about their sins.

41

Literally in the Greek, he had "opened his mouth" to them, though in love (RSV). Now he pleads that they will open their hearts to him (6:13; 7:2).

Cooperate with Your Pastor, Not with Pagans (6:14–7:1)

The next verses just don't seem to belong here. Read 2 Corinthians 6:11–13 and then skip to 7:2. Nothing seems to be left out; 7:2 picks up exactly on what 6:13 was saying. Many, many students of 2 Corinthians believe that some copyist found 6:14–7:1 and, wanting to make sure those words did not get lost, inserted them here. They may not even have been written by Paul. Nevertheless, they are here now, and some believe that they were here from the first.

Perhaps the idea that caused someone to insert them at this point, or Paul to write them here, is the concept of partnership. He has written that they are to work together with him in mission. Now, he says, "Do not be mismatched with unbelievers" (6:14). The RSV translates this as "mismated," and many have interpreted Paul's words as primarily urging Christians not to marry non-Christians. Paul certainly would urge Christians to pick wives and husbands carefully. He had earlier told the Corinthians, however, not to leave their unbelieving marriage partners (1 Cor. 7:13). Paul is not here writing primarily about marriage. He is certainly not writing to promote church schisms, though these words have been used that way! He knows quite well that Christians must and should associate every day with people who are not Christians. As he made and sold tents, he probably did not give a theological examination to all his prospective customers!

"In a postmodern age, the language of sin and salvation will only communicate with the disillusioned if it is absolutely truthful about the realities of their lives, and if it supports them to name those realities for themselves. The days are long gone when most preachers can stand up in pulpits and name people's sins for them. They do not have that authority anymore. What they can do, I believe, is to describe the experience of sin and its aftermath so vividly that people can identify its presence in their own lives, not as a chronic source of guilt, nor as sure proof that they are inherently bad, but as the part of their individual and corporate lives that is crying out for change."—Barbara Brown Taylor, *Speaking of Sin* (Boston: Cowley Publications, 2000), 29.

You may have seen those good people the Amish, their women in bonnets and long dresses, their men with beards, driving buggies. They bear witness that Christians are to be separate, distinctive, different. Christians are to be "saints," "holy"—the idea behind that word is "separate." Yet old-fashioned dress and buggies are not what Paul means.

A key concept is in that word "mismatched." Look at Deuteronomy 22:10 for a possible source. There the prohibition has to do with plowing with an ox and an ass yoked together. It is about work. We are never to associate with non-Christians in tasks that are contrary to our mission. I know a family man who quit his good-paying job. A Christian just could not work in a firm that was cutting corners like that, he explained. There are hints in what Paul says that he is thinking particularly of two things: sexual immorality and temple worship. You may think of other examples of things others do and places others go that members of God's family (2 Cor. 6:18) will carefully avoid. Note the promise for those who will dare to be different (v. 16).

The Joy of Reconciliation (7:2–7)

This letter is confusing; no wonder some believe it is made up of fragments of perhaps seven different letters. In the first two chapters we seem to be in the middle of a story. Paul had been almost frantic to hear about the results of a severe letter he had sent. He had quit waiting for his messenger, Titus, to return and had set out himself, probably from Ephesus. Suddenly he gives a shout of joy, "Thanks be to God[!]" (2:14). We are left to suppose that he had found Titus and received good news, but he doesn't say so. For four chapters all that story seems to be left behind. Now it suddenly resumes. Look back at 2 Corinthians 1:3–7 and at 2:1–4, 12–14, and see how chapter 7 ties in with those verses. Reunited, Titus has brought him the good news of reconciliation. Note how the word "consolation"—or "comfort" or "encouragement"—recurs. Now at last the story seems to have a happy ending.

We are to be ambassadors of reconciliation. Now Paul and the congregation at Corinth are experiencing reconciliation

Jesus' resurrection makes our reconciliation possible.

themselves. "I am overjoyed," Paul writes (7:4). A couple came to a godly lawyer I know. "Help celebrate our anniversary," they told him. "Of what?" he asked. "Exactly ten years ago today we came to you asking for a divorce. You talked us out of it and helped us reconcile. We will never forget that day!" Reconciliation of parent and child, husband and wife, estranged friends, and people within the church reflects the joy of the reconciliation that Christ died to win for us.

Reconciliation and Good Grief (7:8–16)

Reconciliation does not come easy. At Corinth it came about through "godly grief." Obeying Paul, the congregation evidently censured one member, and they and the trouble-maker grieved. Grief is real and in a sense it is never good. Pain is pain, and Paul is sorry that he had to inflict it on his beloved "children" (7:8–9). There is a difference, however, between "godly grief" and "worldly grief" (v. 10). Their godly grief led to repentance and thus to reconciliation. Read verse 11 to see how completely they had repented.

Often in the revival meetings of 150 years ago there would be a "mourner's bench" where someone newly aware of sin might weep and seek God's forgiveness. In your church you may read each Sunday a prayer of confession, but probably few tears are shed. We sing many hymns based on psalms, but they are almost always songs of joyful praise. In the Bible's book of Psalms, however, the largest category is the psalms of lament. Psalmists in pain even cry out in anger at God, "Wake up!" (Ps. 44:23; 59:4–5). Such godly grief is grief that brings its frustration to God, even when God seems not to hear. In fact, there can be no salvation apart from pain, the pain of repentance, no joyful reconciliation without grief for sin, no crown without a cross.

Want to Know More?

About "good grief"? See Robert L. Short, *The Gospel According to Peanuts*, reissued ed. (Louisville, Ky.: Westminster John Knox Press, 2000), especially the chapter titled "Good Grief"; C. S. Lewis, *The Problem of Pain*, reissued ed. (San Francisco: HarperSanFrancisco, 2001); Shirley C. Guthrie Jr., *Christian Doctrine*, rev. ed. (Louisville, Ky.: Westminster John Knox Press, 1994), especially the chapter titled "Why Doesn't God Do Something about It?"

About places mentioned in this epistle such as Corinth, Troas, Macedonia, and Achaia? Try any of these names on the Web, or look them up in any good Bible atlas, such as Herbert Gordon May, ed., *Oxford Bible Atlas*, 3d ed. (London: Oxford University Press, 1985).

About the Amish? Type in "Amish" on the Web for information about why they are different.

Charlie Brown, the protagonist in the late Charles Shultz's comic strip *Peanuts,* used to cry, "Good grief!" Grief that makes us aware of our dependence on God, grief that leads to repentance and reconciliation, is godly grief—good grief indeed.

Chapter 7 brings to an end the first major section of 2 Corinthians. It ends with joy. Paul's joy is even greater because Titus shares it, too (7:13). Paul can express confidence in his spiritual children (v. 10). (He may, like most parents, be encouraging them by expressing more confidence than he really feels.) He can brag on that church. Reconciliation has taken place.

> "'Good grief' may seem to be a contradiction in terms. But actually there are two distinct types of grief—good and not-so-good grief. 'For godly grief produces a repentance that leads to salvation and brings no regret, but worldly grief produces death' (2 Cor. 7:10). Consequently, Christians can call the day on which Christ was crucified 'Good Friday.' For just as the cross was the shadow through which Christ had to pass in order to overcome death, suffering is also the necessary path for any man who wishes 'to walk in newness of life.' 'The way of Christ' is 'the way of the cross'—his cross *and our own.*"—Robert L. Short, *The Gospel According to Peanuts,* reissued ed. (Louisville, Ky.: Westminster John Knox Press, 2000), 82. (The italics are in the original.)

? Questions for Reflection

1. Typical of most "mainline" denominations, the Presbyterian Church (U.S.A.) teaches that Jesus Christ is the only Savior of the world. Yet *Presbyterians Today* (July/August 2002) reports that half of active Presbyterians believe that all religions are "equally good ways of helping a person find ultimate truth." How much urgency do you and your church feel to be ambassadors of Christ, spreading the news of reconciliation through Christ to people around you and to the world? How much should you feel, and what should you do about it?
2. Christians are to be "holy," separate, distinct in many, many ways. How should Christians be different in what they eat, what they drink, what entertainment they enjoy, how they dress, and how they keep the Sabbath? In what other ways should they be different from their non-Christian neighbors?
3. What have you experienced, or what have you observed, of "good grief" or "godly grief"?
4. Chapter 7 ends a major section of 2 Corinthians, and it is approximately halfway through the epistle. This would be a good time to review, asking, What in these chapters has meant most to you so far?

7

2 Corinthians 8:1–9:15

Good News about Giving

An oft-quoted appeal for funds is that of the church treasurer who presented the new church budget to the congregation. The budget included new, exciting items, and as he enthusiastically described each one, he reassured the congregation, "The good news is that we have plenty of money for that great new project." At the end of his appeal, he simply stated, "The bad news is that that money is still in our pockets."

For Paul the opportunity for giving was always good news. Second Corinthians 8–9 is probably the most inspired and inspiring fund-raising message ever penned. Here are some of its verses that have been favorites down through the centuries:

- "[T]hey gave themselves first" (8:5).
- "[Y]ou know the generous act of our Lord Jesus Christ, that though he was rich, yet for your sakes he became poor, so that by his poverty you might become rich" (8:9).
- "God loves a cheerful giver" (9:7).
- "Thanks be to God for his indescribable gift!" (9:15).

Paul probably had mixed motives in wanting to take money to the poor in Jerusalem. He genuinely wanted to help the poor. He wanted the mother church there, made up of Jewish Christians, to see how truly Christian these Gentile converts were. He certainly wanted these gifts to be a Christian witness to Jews. To raise this money he uses every kind of appeal he can think of.

Good News of the Example of the Macedonians (8:1–7)

Paul has good news about the Corinthians' sisters and brothers to the north, the Macedonian Christians. In spite of "severe ordeal" (prob-

ably persecution) and "extreme poverty," "their abundant joy" has "overflowed in a wealth of generosity" (8:2).

My seminary refuses to print reports of alumni's gifts, believing that comparisons provide an unworthy motive, but my college has no such inhibitions. The alumni journal classifies us givers as those who gave in this or that monetary bracket, with the thought that I will be embarrassed to have it printed that I

Christian generosity stems from gratitude for God's good gifts to us.

give less than some classmate. Paul is not above using the good example of the generosity of the Macedonians to encourage the Corinthians, but he does not list amounts. He simply says that "they voluntarily gave according to their means, and even beyond their means" (8:3). Poor as they were, they even begged for the privilege (v. 4)! The key to their generosity is this: "[T]hey gave themselves first" (v. 5). They put themselves on that offering plate (compare Rom. 12:1). Inspired by that example, he hopes the Corinthians will do the same.

Good News of Christ's Loving Example (8:8–15)

Of course, the only standard for "testing" (2 Cor. 8:8) ourselves is not others but Jesus Christ. Our Lord had all the treasure of heaven. He gave it up, gave himself up, even to death, that we might have heavenly riches, new life, eternal life (v. 9).

> "Genuine giving never works by rules and Paul never kept rules! . . . Here is no careful consideration by Christ of the proportion to be given out of what he had and no expectation that in his need he would receive from those to whom he was giving."—Best, *Second Corinthians*, Interpretation, 80.

If J. B. Phillips's paraphrase of verse 10 is correct, it was the Corinthians who had originated the whole idea of this offering. Now,

Want to Know More?

About Church World Service? Write them at P.O. Box 968, Elkhart, IN 46515, or enter "Church World Service" on the Web.

About your denomination's stewardship program? The Web will give you the address of your denomination's headquarters, and your pastor can give it to you also.

About where your money goes? Most mainline denominations produce a mission study guide or similar booklet each year. Write for a copy. The example of others will inspire you!

Paul says, they must match their original eagerness by completing what they had begun (v. 11). Give, Paul says, as you are able. The goal is that there should be a "fair balance" (v. 13). Presbyterian minister and author Don Shriver tells about startling a group of Christian industrialists. He proposed that a Christian would measure our economy not by the total wealth of our nation but by how well we share. The bottom line is not the gross national product but how well off our poorest citizens are, especially in comparison with others. Paul himself determines the bottom line, if not quite by equality, at least by that kind of "balance."

Paul sees God as originating the concept of balance. Behind 2 Corinthians 8:15 is a story. When God rained down manna on the Israelites in the wilderness the command was that each should gather enough, but no more. Some tried to hoard an extra supply, but at the end of the day the misers had no more than the rest (Exod. 16:18).

Good News about the Administration of Their Gifts (8:16–24)

Paul assures the Corinthians that there will be no chance of misappropriation of their gifts. A committee of people they know, headed not by Paul but by Titus, will see that the money goes where they intend.

Last night's evening news reported scandalous misappropriation of funds in a highly respected charity. Tragically, millions of Christians give money to independent "Christian" ministries over which they have no control—money that would have been far more wisely spent through their denominational agencies. Through democratic procedures you have chosen your denomination's businesspeople, who are directly responsible to and governed by you who give the money. Some years ago a survey was made of relief programs. Among the largest, the most efficient—that is, the one in which the largest amount of money went not for overhead but actually to help the needy—was Church World Service, under the cooperative control of mainline Protestant denominations. Paul promises such responsible management to the Corinthians.

Avoid the Bad News of Embarrassment (9:1–5)

Not always successfully, Paul almost always tries to be positive. "It is not necessary for me to write you about the ministry to the saints," he flatters them (9:1). Actually, he has just written them a whole chapter, and now he writes another! He wants to be certain that they do make their promised gift.

> "When it comes to giving, some people stop at nothing."—attributed to Jimmy Carter.

Paul had gone out on a limb. When the Corinthians had pledged a large gift, he had bragged to the Macedonians about it, helping inspire in them their amazing generosity (9:2). Now what a letdown it will be if Paul comes and finds that the Corinthians had not given as he had promised the Macedonians they would. He, the appointed supervisors, and the Corinthians themselves would be "humiliated" (v. 4). So he is sending the committee and this letter to make sure that all is given before Paul arrives for his promised visit.

The Best News: God Gives in Love (9:6–15)

The loving God, Paul assures us, will reward our giving "bountifully" (9:6). The more generous we are, the more we will be open to the gifts God wants to give us. Paul does not mean, as some preachers and popular books have proposed, that generosity is the way to "success." Many mothers have starved as they gave their last bit of food to their children. Our giving can reflect the joyful nature of our generous God, however, for "God loves a cheerful giver" (v. 7). The word translated "cheerful" is the Greek from which we get the word "hilarious."

God is a "hilarious" giver, one who "gives to the poor" (9:9). God "scatters" gifts, broadcasting them to the evil and the good. Study 2 Corinthians 9:6–15 to see the promises this God makes to those who give, not in the hope of getting, but out of the joy of giving in itself.

There is a kind of inspired double-talk in verse 12. The word Paul uses here for "ministry" can also be translated "worship." It is like our word "service," which also carries both meanings. Some church bulletins end each Sunday with the sentence "The service begins when the worship is over." Worship is service, too, so the sentence is not quite correct. Our service, our giving, "supplies the needs of the saints but also overflows with many thanksgivings to God" (v. 12). Singing and praying are acts of worship, and so is putting money in the offering plate. By giving, "you glorify God" (v. 13). "Hilarious" giving is an act of praise, and it is contagious. It spreads praise and thanksgiving everywhere to God (vv. 13–14).

> "When a poor person dies of hunger, it has not happened because God did not take care of him or her. It has happened because neither you nor I wanted to give that person what he or she needed."—Mother Teresa.

There are, then, glorious results from giving. Paul never really wants people to give because of what they will get out of it, though, even when they recognize that what they will get is great spiritual rewards, not material rewards. The reason we are to give is in gratitude for what God has already given to us. Thus Paul builds to a climax with his shout of praise, "Thanks be to God for his indescribable gift!" (v. 15).

? Questions for Reflection

1. Paul uses every kind of persuasion he can think of to encourage the Corinthians to give—some of them perhaps not of the very highest kind. See how many different motives you can find Paul appealing to in 2 Corinthians 8–9. Which motives are best?
2. These two chapters abound in delightful, meaningful verses. Read them again and see which verses are your favorites.
3. Paul says that "you will be enriched in every way" (9:11). That is just not true—not literally. What truth is there, then, in that promise? What are the rewards of giving?
4. Take a look at your own congregation's budget and its giving. Try writing the letter you imagine Paul might write to you and others about your church's stewardship.

2 Corinthians 10:1-11:29   8

The Authority of a "Fool"

Few people name the last chapters of 2 Corinthians among their favorite Bible passages. Sunday lectionary readings tend to skip 2 Corinthians 10 completely. As Paul writes chapters 10–13 he is angry and sarcastic. Nevertheless the issue involved in the last chapters of 2 Corinthians, the authority of Paul, is as basic to our own faith as it was to the Corinthians. The authority of the New Testament is bound up with the inspiration of its most prolific author, the apostle Paul.

The angry tone of 2 Corinthians 10–13 is so different from that of the earlier chapters that most students of 2 Corinthians believe that they are part of a different epistle. Perhaps these chapters come from the severe letter he had written, with tears, referred to in 2 Corinthians 2:3–4. Most scholars think they come from a later time, designed to put down yet another revolt in that always contentious congregation at Corinth. Paul pleads, argues, boasts, and threatens. The fact that his words are preserved suggests that, at least with some, Paul won the battle.

Paul Fights a Different Kind of War (10:1-6)

Paul begins by assuring his readers that he intends to be pleading with "the meekness and gentleness of Christ" (10:1). (Of course, Jesus could let loose some fiery denunciations of his enemies, too, as in Matt. 23:13–36.) Indeed, when Paul was in Corinth, he was so meek and gentle that his rivals could make fun of his humility. Among ancient Romans a leader was supposed to be bold, proud, even haughty, not humble. Nevertheless Paul assures the Corinthians that

51

a war is on and that, humble as he is, he is leading the fight (2 Cor. 10:2–3). With divine power he will use superhuman weapons to "destroy strongholds" (v. 4). Hymns like "Onward Christian Soldiers" have been omitted from some modern hymnals because the church has too often sanctioned war. In Paul's quite different situation, however, Paul can and does use military figures of speech (compare Eph. 6:11–17).

> "Satan is at war with humanity and one stratagem in war is to wear the enemy's uniform; in that way his lines can be penetrated and destroyed from within. More danger has always lain for the church in inner corruption than in outer persecution."—Best, *Second Corinthians*, Interpretation, 108.

Paul's is, however, a different kind of war. Paul is a sort of "headhunter." He is out to conquer minds, to persuade, to "destroy arguments" (2 Cor. 10:4), and to "take every thought captive" to Christ (v. 5). When he returns to Corinth he will even be willing to apply the church's discipline to the disobedient (v. 6).

The Basis of Paul's Authority (10:7–18)

Now Paul begins his defense. Some evangelists have newly arrived in Corinth. They have been bragging that they are superior to Paul, and reading between the lines we can tell something of what they claimed. These newcomers boast that they truly "belong to Christ." To realize that Paul belongs to Christ too, all the Corinthians have to do, Paul says, is to look at him and the life he has led before their own eyes (10:7). His enemies charge that though Paul writes bold letters, he is weak and vacillating when he is with them (vv. 8–11). His answer: Just wait until I get there, and you will see that I can back up my words with actions!

With sarcasm Paul says that he would not think of comparing himself with these newcomers. They tell everyone how great they are as they "commend themselves," comparing themselves with each other—a stupid standard (10:12)! Paul is going to boast, but he will keep his claims within double limits. First, he will claim authority only in the churches he feels have been assigned to him, places where he was first to bring the gospel. These intruders have been stealing Paul's sheep, preaching "in someone else's [Paul's] sphere of action" (v. 16). Far from invading another minister's parish, Paul hopes that the Corinthians will so grow in faith that he can move on to establish other churches in places no Christian missionary has been before

(vv. 13–16). The second limit on his claims is that the only boast he makes is not selfish. Instead he will "boast in the Lord" (vv. 17–18). I think of the preacher who began a sermon by announcing, "For the next thirty minutes I am just going to brag about Jesus."

Paul Is a Jealous Father (11:1–15)

Now Paul's figure of speech is no longer war-based; instead, he pictures himself as a jealous father guarding his daughter from a seducer. The figure of God's people as married to God is as old as the prophet Hosea and is as eternal as Revelation (compare Hos. 2:16; Rev. 21:2). Paul was the first to bring the Corinthians the gospel (2 Cor. 10:14); he was their father in the faith. His goal was to present them to Christ as a father gives the bride to her husband, "a chaste virgin" (11:1–2). Building on the Jewish legend that Satan sexually seduced Eve, he compares these intruders in Corinth to "cunning" seduc-

> Let us rejoice and exult
> and give him the glory,
> for the marriage of the Lamb has come,
> and his bride has made herself ready;
> to her it has been granted to be clothed
> with fine linen, bright and pure.
> —Revelation 19:7–8.

ers of the bride of Christ (v. 3). That is, they are preaching a different Jesus, a different spirit, and a different gospel from the one Paul had proclaimed (v. 4). Yet the Corinthians seem ready to accept the newest thing that comes along. Paul's bitterness shows through as he sarcastically calls these false evangelists "super-apostles." He says, in effect, "Okay, so I am not as good a preacher as any of them. But when it comes to knowing the Lord, you have seen for yourselves what I am" (vv. 5–6).

The people in Corinth were not the last to be seduced. In the comic strip *Doonesbury* a few years ago, "Rev. Sloan" was showing some newcomers around his church. The husband seemed impressed by this pastor and the congregation's ministry. The wife, however, was hesitant. The church in the next block has a larger gymnasium, she reminded her husband. Today glamourous preachers, pulpit oratory, bright lights, big crowds, and new, faddish sects compete with churches whose appeal is only the same old good news about our Lord.

Of all the charges against Paul, the one that seems the oddest to us is the complaint that Paul preached the gospel free of charge (11:7–11). (One suspects that his competitors did not make that mistake!) Paul had earned his own living as a tent-maker. Historians of sociology help us to understand how this made Paul seem unworthy. They tell us that in Greco-Roman class-conscious culture, a client was supposed to accept favors and offices from his patron, but in return to acknowledge his obligation to his benefactor. Paul, his rivals must have claimed, refused money so that he would feel free of any obligation to the Corinthians. Paul's real goal, of course, was "to refrain from burdening" the church (v. 9), and he was proud of it (v. 10). Was it "because I do not love you? God knows I do!" (v. 11). Many of us still tend to measure success in terms of income rather than service.

With his anger boiling over, Paul denounces his rivals as "boasters . . . false apostles, [and] deceitful workers" (v. 13). They are like Satan, who "can disguise himself as an angel of light" (11:14). God will punish them (v. 15)!

The Case for the "Fool" (11:16–29)

Paul feels like a fool. As a humble man, the one thing he does not want to do is to brag about himself. Having now answered the charges against him, however, he feels forced to try to argue a case that he does have God-given authority.

Boasting, he knows, is foolish, but, with irony and sarcasm again, he says that the Corinthians seem to prefer fools. That being the case, he says in effect, "I will be a fool, too, and do some bragging of my own" (11:16–21). Thus pressured, he lists his qualifications.

Apparently his rivals claimed to be better Jews than he, so he notes his own pure Jewishness (11:22; compare Phil. 3:4–5). More importantly, he affirms his own status as a minister of Christ (2 Cor. 11:23). The clearest way for them to see his commitment as a Christian minister, however, is for him to recount some of the things that he has gone through to fulfill his calling. Paul then apologizes again, admitting that he is not here speaking the word of the Lord and is in fact speaking madness by

When, near the end of the first century, once again false teachers threatened the faithfulness of the Corinthian church, Bishop Clement of Rome reminded them: "Because of jealousy and strife Paul pointed the way to the reward of endurance; seven times he was imprisoned, he was exiled, he was stoned, he was a preacher in both east and west, and won great renown for his faith, teaching uprightness to the whole world, and reaching the farthest limit of the west, and bearing a martyr's witness before the rulers he passed out of the world and was taken up into the holy place, having proved a very great example of endurance."—The First Letter of Clement 5.7, as found in Edgar J. Goodspeed, The Apostolic Fathers: An American Translation (New York: Harper & Brothers, Publishers, 1950), 52.

such human boasting (vv. 17, 23). Can any of his rivals match this, though? With that thought, he reels off some of the things he has endured as he has traveled over the Mediterranean world preaching (vv. 23–29).

Was there ever another autobiography like this one? Paul does some counting for us. (For your part, you might count how many times he uses the word "danger.") Deuteronomy 25:2–3 prescribed a Jewish punishment of forty blows with a whip; to make sure that they did not go beyond forty they would stop at thirty-nine. Paul received this kind of flogging five times (2 Cor. 11:24). The beating with rods implies punishment by Romans, inflicted three times even though Paul was a Roman citizen.

Read on in these verses. What different kinds of danger can you find in Paul's account? List, too, the different kinds of hardship he endured. Acts gives us an account of some of what Paul went through for us, but obviously it does not tell nearly all the story. Consider what sort of physical condition he must have been in by the time he had gone through all this!

Yet the apostle ends his summary of sufferings not with anything physical. Some readers know the kind of thing Paul means when he writes of "daily pressure" and "anxiety" about his work. His anxiety comes from the heart of a loving pastor, who identifies in every way with the people of his beloved congregation (11:29). Burnout is an occupational hazard of ministry.

 Want to Know More?

About the Apostle Paul? See James S. Stewart, *A Man in Christ: The Vital Elements of St. Paul's Religion* (London: Hodder and Stoughton Limited, 1935); Edgar J. Goodspeed, *Paul*, reissued ed. (Nashville: Abingdon Press, 1980).

About the authority of creeds and scripture? See Shirley C. Guthrie Jr., *Christian Doctrine*, rev. ed. (Louisville, Ky.: Westminster John Knox Press, 1994), chapters 1–2; John H. Leith, *Basic Christian Doctrine* (Louisville, Ky.: Westminster/John Knox Press, 1993), chapter 20.

About new sects—and ancient religions, newly popular? Check the Web sites with names such as "New Age," "Hari Krishna," "Nation of Islam," and "Mega-churches."

Nowhere else does Paul give such an account of what he has gone through to bring all of us the gospel. In the situation in Corinth, reluctantly and feeling like a fool as he does it, Paul feels forced to admit that he has endured all these things. We can be glad that he did! Christians have always said that Paul's words in his writings are inspired. There was inspiration in Paul's life, too. His example has inspired others, down through the ages, to answer the call of Christ, no matter what it may cost.

? Questions for Reflection

1. Suppose a committee recommended that your congregation accept as pastor a man or woman who was just like Paul. How would your congregation respond? How would you? What qualities make him fit to be pastor or might make people hesitant to accept him?

2. There are many competing Christian churches and many non-Christian sects that attract more and more people. Suppose you moved to another city; on what basis *would* you choose a church, and on what basis *should* you choose a church?

3. Paul is writing to defend his authority. We take his epistles as part of our authoritative book, the Bible. What are the bases of this authority? Why do you believe that Paul's letters are part of the "word of God written"?

4. Often a good way to study a passage is to look for repeated words and ideas. What repeated words or ideas do you find in 2 Corinthians 10:1–11:29? What does Paul say about those things, and what does that mean for us?

9

Powerful Weaklings

Paul revels in a kind of divine double-talk. Repeatedly he affirms that two opposite things are both true. (The theological name for such seeming contradictions is *paradox*.) Paul says that we are pre-destined, but he also says that we are morally responsible. He says that each person must bear his own burden, but he says that we must bear each other's burdens. He says that we are saved by grace alone, not by works, but that we must work out our own salvation. He says that Jesus was crucified, but he is alive forevermore. And here he writes one of the oddest contradictions one could imagine: "whenever I am weak, then I am strong" (2 Cor. 12:10).

Bragging about Weakness (11:30–33)

Paul has been forced to defend himself. He doesn't want to boast and he feels like a fool doing it, but to defend his gospel he has to defend himself. Thus he has described the dangers and difficulties he has gone through to bring us that gospel (11:23–29). He ended his remarkable autobiography with a confession of his pastoral care and concern, his "anxiety" for and identification with the people in the congregations he has founded: "Who is weak, and I am not weak? Who is made to stumble, and I am not indignant?" (v. 28).

Now he picks up on the word "weak" and milks it for all the nourishment he can give us from it. "If I must boast, I will boast of the things that show my weakness" (11:30). He has recounted stories of endurance that might make him appear to be claiming to

"Sometimes when we attempt to teach others a new technique or skill (e.g., a grown-up with a child), we find they obstinately resist our instruction, thinking they know it all. It is then impossible to help them. But once they recognize their 'weakness,' we can come in with our 'strength.' So God cannot impart strength to us until we acknowledge our weakness. It was Paul's weakness in respect to the thorn in the flesh about which he could do nothing that led him to allow God in with his strength."—Best, *Second Corinthians*, Interpretation, 120–21.

be a courageous hero. So he quickly recalls a story to present himself in a most unheroic light. Powerful people ran Paul out of town. Compare Acts 9:23–25. What could be more ridiculous, even comic? What could show more clearly that Paul was nothing in himself than this spectacle of him forced to escape for his life by being let down over the city wall, crammed into a basket! In myself, I am nothing, Paul is saying, but he will go on to "boast" that in Christ one may in a different way be strong indeed.

An Indescribable Spiritual "High" (12:1–6)

Second Corinthians 11–12 take us on a kind of spiritual roller-coaster. Paul boasts his credentials as an aristocratic Hebrew (2 Cor. 11:22). Then he tells about having to undergo all kinds of dangers (vv. 23–29), but enduring them all like a hero. He follows with his comic letdown at Damascus. Now he tells about how it was given to him to experience being lifted up to paradise itself (12:1–6). (In the next verses he is going to tell how jarringly he was brought back to earth.)

If Paul himself cannot describe it, obviously we cannot know just what his vision was. Repeatedly Acts tells of Paul having some important spiritual experience, perhaps a vision or an inspired dream (Acts 9:2–6; 16:9; 22:17–21; 27:23). Paul was, indeed, a "mystic," that is, a person who at times has a direct, extrasensory experience of the divine. Two things about Paul's transcendent vision may be emphasized:

1. This experience was real and deeply meaningful for Paul. It should indeed reassure us. We have not had such an experience, but Paul really did. We gain faith from knowing that other saints down through history, some famous and some of whom few ever hear, really have had true and meaningful times of unique awareness of God.

2. Paul never describes this kind of vision as normal for most true Christians. He tells about it only to refute his enemies. "You want visions?" he says in effect. "I'll give you visions. Try to match this one!" He is reluctant and almost stuttering on paper, however, as he writes about it. Nowhere else does he describe it; far less does he tell

us to try for such a vision or regard it, or lack of it, as a sign of our standing with the Lord. Some forms of Hinduism place more emphasis on individual mystic experiences than does Christianity. Catholics have been more given to mysticism than have Protestants, with medieval saints often telling of visions, especially of the Virgin Mary. Protestants' experience of God is almost always a mediated experience, awareness of Christ and God's truth mediated through the sacraments, through the Bible, through sermons, through Christian friends, and through groups like the one with whom—I hope—you may be studying 2 Corinthians.

The great truth for us here is that God does speak—in various ways, but really does speak—to us and lift our spirits. In the end God will lift even us to paradise.

Dropped Back Down to Earth, Hard (12:7–8)

One thing that keeps even the most holy saints humble is this: Spiritual "highs" are often followed by spiritual "lows." Paul was brought back down to earth with a double blow. First, he had a "thorn in the flesh." Paul never tells us exactly what that means. Calvin thinks Paul refers here to some special kind of spiritual temptation. Perhaps sexual temptation or depression afflicted Paul. Most commentators think Paul means some physical infirmity. Anybody who had been beaten so often was bound to have some resulting lameness. Perhaps he means eye trouble. He was struck blind once (Acts 9:8). He reminds the Galatians that once they would have pulled out their eyes to give him (Gal. 4:12–15). He usually dictated his letters, and when he wrote he did so with large letters (Gal. 6:11). Perhaps it is just as well that we don't know what Paul's affliction was; we know our own.

He was also brought down to earth by the fact that though he prayed repeatedly and earnestly the "thorn in the

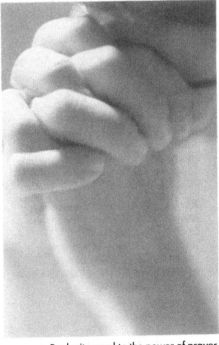

Paul witnessed to the power of prayer.

59

flesh" stayed right there. Did he not pray in faith? Of course Paul had faith! Did not Jesus say, "Whatever you ask for in prayer with faith, you will receive it" (Matt. 21:22)? (Perhaps you will find that Luke understood Jesus' meaning more completely if you read what he records in Luke 11:13.) There is truth in the old adage "Be careful what you pray for; you just may get it." God does often, sometimes it seems almost miraculously, give us exactly what we pray for. If you have prayed often enough and hard enough, however, you know that sometimes that just does not happen. Paul certainly found that out!

> "Prayer is an application of faith to the particular circumstances of the moment."—Perry LeFevre, *Understandings of Prayer* (Philadelphia: Westminster Press, 1981), 24.

Paul says that God worked out a purpose in Paul's "thorn in the flesh" and the failure of his prayer to get what he asked: It was to keep him humble (2 Cor. 12:7).

In Our Weakness, God's Power (12:9–10)

God did answer Paul's prayer, and what an answer! "My grace is sufficient for you, for [my] power is made perfect in weakness" (12:9). The Greek word Paul uses for power gives us our word *dynamite*. That dynamite was power enough. "Yes," Paul says, "I am a weakling. But somehow that is all right; I can rest in the awesome power of God." Paul will even brag about his weakness because it shows so clearly that whatever good he has accomplished is entirely the work of Jesus Christ (11:9–10).

Want to Know More?

About prayer? See Perry LeFevre, *Understandings of Prayer* (Philadelphia: Westminster Press, 1981); George Arthur Buttrick, *Prayer*, reissued ed. (Nashville: Abingdon Press, 1977). For guidance in your own daily prayer, try *These Days*, published quarterly by Presbyterian Publishing (available by calling 1-800-227-2872).

About grief and "unanswered" prayer? Read C. S. Lewis, *The Problem of Evil* (New York: Macmillan, 1962); C. S. Lewis, *A Grief Observed*, reissued ed. (San Francisco: HarperSanFrancisco, 2001); Reynolds Price, *A Whole New Life* (New York: Atheneum, 1994).

I spoke of this passage to a physical therapist who works sixty hours a week providing help for people with twisted, misshapen bodies. "Have you seen people who are weak in body but have that inner strength?" I asked. "Oh yes," she said. "Oh yes!"

Cancer of the spine has for years confined to a wheelchair award-winning novelist Reynolds Price. He tells of a mystic experience in which Christ summoned him to follow and then baptized him in the Sea of Galilee. "Your sins are forgiven," Jesus announced. Price raised the question that at the time bothered him much more, "Am I also cured?" "That, too," Jesus replied. Price is still in the wheelchair, and every day is a battle with pain. Yet remembering that experience he has been able to receive what he calls "A Whole New Life" (which he describes in his book of the same name).

> "Nothing, no matter how severe, can happen for which God does not also provide a way out, a new exodus (1 Cor. 10:13). No simpler formulation of the good news is possible: God's grace is sufficient. Period."
> —Sampley, *The New Interpreter's Bible*, vol. 11, 166.

"Whenever I am weak, I am strong" (12:10). Paul knows one other, more important illustration of that mind-boggling paradox: Jesus "was crucified in weakness, but lives by the power of God" (13:4).

? Questions for Reflection

1. "Our extremity is God's opportunity." What humiliating experience have you had that you can laugh at now, an experience that may have been helpful in the long run though painful at the time?
2. Paul had an extrasensory vision of paradise. Most of us have not had such an experience, but sense the divine only in a mediated way. When and through what means have you been most aware of God?
3. What experience have you had of answered prayer? Was the answer the one you expected?
4. Whom can you tell about who seems to show the truth of Paul's paradox that God's strength is made perfect in weakness?

10 2 Corinthians 12:11–13:13

The Last Words: Grace, Love, and Communion

Second Corinthians is really a kind of love letter. It is not a romantic love letter, of course; it is the love letter of a father to a wayward child. Paul is sometimes angry, sarcastic, and dictatorial, but he is writing to people he loves. If in this letter, as an ancient description of Paul admitted, he sometimes "looked like a man," in the last two, stern chapters of this letter there are still moments where how he also "looked like an angel" shines through.

The Defense Rests (12:11–21)

I get the feeling that Paul is exhausted. Paragraph after paragraph, he has pleaded, bragged, apologized for bragging, attacked, begged, and defended himself in every way he can think of. Feeling like a fool in doing so still, he resumes his defense (12:11). Did Paul really do the miracles described in Acts? The Corinthians could not doubt it; they had seen with their own eyes how, when he was with them, God—he does not say Paul—performed "signs and wonders and mighty works" (12:12). "Signs" point to something, "wonders" are acts that amaze, and "mighty works" display God's power. How can they doubt that he is a true apostle?

> "The best defense is a good offense."— football coaches' maxim.

With irony he apologizes for not accepting money from them (12:13). Maybe, his rivals suggest, since he did not accept pay, he was scooping off money from the church treasury. His refusal to be dependent on them, however, was like a father not wanting to be dependent on his children (12:14). Far from stealing their money, "I will most gladly spend and be spent for you" (v. 15). What grieves him so is that he has loved them even more than his other churches; he had stayed in Corinth longer than in most of the cities (v. 15; compare Acts 18:11). They surely knew they could trust his partner Titus. It was Titus and a friend, not Paul, who were handling the money being raised for the poor (2 Cor. 12:16–18).

As he draws to an end of his defense, Paul wants to make one thing clear: God, not the Corinthians, is the one to test him (12:19). What worries Paul is not fear that he has not been a true apostle. It is that when he comes to Corinth again he is going to find those new Christians reverting to the sinful lives they lived before they were baptized (vv. 20–21).

Warning: Paul Is Coming Soon (13:1–4)

Acts 18 tells us about Paul's first sojourn in Corinth. Later he made the "painful visit" referred to in 2 Corinthians 2:1. The purpose of chapters 10–13 is now clear: Paul is preparing the Corinthians for a third visit. Three visits will be like the three witnesses that Deuteronomy 19:15 said bring conviction. In effect, Paul says, "There will be no more 'Mr. Nice Guy.' You want proof that I am an apostle? I'll give you proof of a kind you won't like unless you straighten up. Christ was crucified in weakness, but Christ will now come with power. You know that power, because it is in you. My rivals say I'm a wimp. Maybe *I* am, but I will come with the power of *Christ*."

The Teacher and the Final Exam (13:5–10)

A university professor I know laughed about a criticism made by one of his students on an evaluation form: "This teacher puts too much responsibility for the learning on the students." Paul warns the Corinthians that they are responsible. "Test . . . test . . . test . . . test . . . test" (2 Cor. 13:5–7)—five times in just three verses Paul uses one or another form of the same Greek word. The Corinthians have been asking for a test or "proof"—the

> "A teacher affects eternity; he can never tell where his influence stops."—Henry Adams, as quoted in *The Great Thoughts*, compiled by George Seldes (New York: Ballantine Books, 1985), 4.

63

same word as in verse 3—that he is an apostle. He hopes that he has not flunked that test. He knows that the real test of a teacher is not how popular he is nor what his student evaluation forms say; it is how much his students have learned. "Test yourselves," he says, like a teacher urging students to imagine exam questions in advance and prepare for tomorrow's exam. They've been testing him long enough; now it is their turn to be tested. There need be and can be no demonstration of his stringent, powerful authority if they are ready to make an "A" on the test (v. 7). He will be delighted if he finds them so strong that he can simply be the weak little man again because he finds that they are on their way toward perfection. Their growth is all he cares about (vv. 9–10).

What It Takes to Pass the Test
(13:11–12)

Most modern translations properly use the word "farewell," even "good-bye," in verse 11. Around A.D. 400, however, Chrysostom noted that the word is, literally, "Rejoice." So he imagined this conversation between a reader and Paul:

> "Thou hast pained, terrified, thrown them into an agony, made them to tremble and fear, and how biddest thou them rejoice?" "Why, for this reason I bid them rejoice. For," [Paul] says, "if what is your part follow upon mine, there will be nothing to prevent that joy. For all my part has been done; I have suffered long, I have delayed, I have forborne to cut off, I have advised, I have alarmed, I have threatened, so as by every means to gather you in unto the fruit of repentance. And now it behooveth that your part be done, and so your joy will be unfading."

That is a good summary of 2 Corinthians 10–13 and Paul's final message in this letter.

Paul's goals for the Corinthians are order, mutual agreement, and peace, all with the blessing of "the God of love" (13:11). A sign of such peace and love is that they should kiss each other. In church apparently men kissed only men, and women only women; we still see that custom in the Middle East. In the second century, in some congregations such kisses were a requirement before one could take communion. In most churches today, we settle for a handshake and the words "the peace of Christ be with you."

The Threefold Benediction (13:13)

For nearly two thousand years ministers have stretched out their arms over their congregations and voiced the benediction with which Paul closes this letter: "The grace of the Lord Jesus Christ, the love of God, and the communion [or fellowship] of the Holy Spirit be with all of you." That blessing, 2 Corinthians 13:13, merits a close look.

It would be anachronistic to read into that triune blessing a full-fledged doctrine of the Trinity. The word "trinity" is not in the New Testament. It was more than a century later that a scholar named Tertullian first used it about the God we worship. This benediction, however, must surely have been one of the many passages in the Bible that caused the church to work out that understanding of the One in whom we believe. The orthodox formula of "one God in three persons" itself becomes heretical if one thinks of the word "person" in the way we ordinarily use that term, as though God were three "people." One helpful but incomplete way to think of the Trinity is that God acts simultaneously in three "roles" in the drama of our salvation, but that fails to describe the reality of the Father loving the Son and the Son loving the Father and the Spirit binding us and them together. The doctrine of the Trinity remains a sacred mystery, but through it we grow in our understanding of the Lord.

Want to Know More?

About the doctrine of the Trinity? See John 14; the Nicene Creed; Shirley C. Guthrie Jr., *Christian Doctrine*, rev. ed. (Louisville, Ky.: Westminster John Knox Press, 1994), chapter 5; John H. Leith, *Basic Christian Doctrine* (Louisville, Ky.: Westminster/John Knox Press, 1993), 46–50; Philip W. Butin, *The Trinity*, Foundations of Christian Faith (Louisville, Ky.: Geneva Press, 2001).

About what happened on Paul's third visit? See Ernest Best, *Second Corinthians*, Interpretation (Atlanta: John Knox Press, 1987), 139.

About living by grace, love, and peace? See *The Study Catechism, Full Version* (Louisville, Ky.: Geneva Press, 1998), questions 2–4.

About 2 Corinthians? See the commentaries in the bibliography on page 69–70.

The emphasis in 2 Corinthians 13:13, however, is probably not so much on the threefold nature of God as on the three words "grace," "love," and "peace." It is in these three that Paul wants to see his "children" growing toward perfection. We use the word *grace* to describe beautiful action; a dancer or a diver moves with grace. Christ is the beautiful action of God. The Greek word for grace—*charis,* from which we get "charismatic" and "charity"—implies goodness and happiness. *Love,* Paul had told the Corinthians in his first letter to them, is "the greatest" thing, even greater than faith and hope (1 Cor. 13:13). For Paul that Greek word, *agape*, refers not to sexual love but to self-giving concern for others, the kind of love our heavenly Father has for us, God's children. The word *koinonia* is sometimes translated "communion" and sometimes "fellowship." It calls to mind the Lord's Supper. Paul is perhaps deliberately ambiguous. "Of the Holy Spirit" means that we actually have communion with God, the divine self—but "of the Holy Spirit" also refers to that fellowship with each other that the Holy Spirit can bring even the feuding Corinthians . . . and even us.

> "The order is significant; the *grace of Christ* expresses and leads one on toward the *love of God*, and the *love of God*, when actualized through the *Spirit*, produces *communion* with God and with one another."
> —Bruce M. Metzger and Roland E. Murphy, eds., *The New Oxford Annotated Bible with the Apocryphal/Deuterocanonical Books* (New York: Oxford University Press, 1991), 262 NT, italics in original.

Paul began both 1 and 2 Corinthians with "grace to you and peace from God our Father and the Lord Jesus Christ." Now he ends with what is sometimes called "the apostolic benediction."

Perhaps this far lesser writer may end this commentary by echoing that great teacher's words for you who have been reading it:

The grace of the Lord Jesus Christ,
the love of God,
and the communion of the Holy Spirit
be with all of you.

? Questions for Reflection

1. Suppose the Apostle Paul plans to visit your church three months from now, looking at its books, the lives of its members, and its missionary endeavor. What preparations would you try to make?
2. Paul writes with the goal of inspiring a kind of fear in the Corinthian congregation. One theologian has said that it is impossible to love God if you have no fear of God. In what way, if any, do you think that is true?
3. Many congregations engage in self-examination by developing a statement of their mission. Many voice a prayer of confession at each worship service. In what ways do these fulfill Paul's com-

mand, "Examine yourselves" (13:5)? How significant are these forms of self-examination, and in what other ways must congregations and individuals examine themselves?

4. We have come to the end of this study of 2 Corinthians. What things in this letter and in this study have meant most to you? What will you do about them?

Bibliography

Barclay, William. *The Letters to the Corinthians.* Rev. ed. Daily Bible Study. Louisville, Ky.: Westminster John Knox Press, 2002.

Best, Ernest. *Second Corinthians.* Interpretation. Atlanta: John Knox Press, 1987.

Bretall, Robert, ed. *A Kierkegaard Anthology.* New York: Modern Library, 1936.

Brownrigg, Ronald. *Who's Who in the New Testament.* New York: Holt, Rinehart & Winston, 1971.

Calvin, John. *Institutes of the Christian Religion.* Trans. John Allen. Philadelphia: Presbyterian Board of Christian Education, n.d.

———. *The Second Epistle of Paul the Apostle to the Corinthians.* Trans. T. A. Smail. Grand Rapids: Wm. B. Eerdmans Publishing Company, 1964. (Calvin's commentaries can be found on the Web at http://www.ccel.org/c/calvin/calcom/calcom.html.)

Chrysostom. *Homilies on Second Corinthians.* Nicene and Post-Nicene Fathers, series 1, vol. 12. Found on the Web at http://www.ccel.org/fathers2NPNF1-12/npnfl-12-80.htm.

Coogan, Michael D., ed. *The New Oxford Annotated Bible, with the Apocryphal/Deuterocanonical Books.* New Revised Standard Version. 3d ed. New York: Oxford University Press, 2001.

Filson, Floyd V., and James Reid. *The Second Epistle to the Corinthians.* Interpreter's Bible 10. Nashville: Abingdon Press, 1953.

Guthrie, Shirley C. Jr. *Christian Doctrine.* Rev. ed. Louisville, Ky.: Westminster John Knox Press, 1994.

LeFevre, Perry. *Understandings of Prayer.* Philadelphia: Westminster Press, 1981.

Leith, John H. *Basic Christian Doctrine.* Louisville, Ky.: Westminster/John Knox Press, 1993.

Lewis, C. S. *The Problem of Pain.* Reissued ed. New York: Touchstone, 1996.

Luther, Martin. *Three Treatises.* Trans. W. A. Lambert. Rev. by Harold J. Grimm. Philadelphia: Fortress Press, 1970.

Metzger, Bruce M., and Roland B. Murphy, eds. *The New Oxford Annotated Bible with the Apocryphal/Deuterocanonical Books.* New Revised Standard Version. New York: Oxford University Press, 1991.

Phillips, J. B. *Letters to Young Churches.* New York: Macmillan, 1957.

Plummer, A. *The Second Epistle of Paul to the Corinthians.* Cambridge: Cambridge University Press, 1923.

Price, Reynolds. *A Whole New Life.* New York: Atheneum, 1994.

Ramsay, William M. *The Westminster Guide to the Books of the Bible.* Louisville, Ky.: Westminster John Knox Press, 1994.

Sampley, J. Paul. *The Second Letter to the Corinthians.* New Interpreter's Bible 11. Nashville: Abingdon Press, 2000.

Short, Robert L. *The Gospel According to Peanuts.* Reissued ed. Louisville, Ky.: Westminster John Knox Press, 2000.

Stewart, James S. *A Man in Christ.* London: Hodder and Stoughton Limited, 1935.

Taylor, Barbara Brown. *Speaking of Sin: The Lost Language of Salvation.* Boston: Cowley Publications, 2000.

Interpretation Bible Studies
Leader's Guide

Interpretation Bible Studies (IBS), for adults and older youth, are flexible, attractive, easy-to-use, and filled with solid information about the Bible. IBS helps Christians discover the guidance and power of the scriptures for living today. Perhaps you are leading a church school class, a mid-week Bible study group, or a youth group meeting, or simply using this in your own personal study. Whatever the setting may be, we hope you find this *Leader's Guide* helpful. Since every context and group is different, this *Leader's Guide* does not presume to tell you how to structure Bible study for your situation. Instead, the *Leader's Guide*

> "The traditioning process, when it is faithful, must be disciplined, critical, and informed by the best intelligence of the day. But it must be continued—and is continued—each time we meet in synagogue or church for telling and sharing, for reading and study, each time we present ourselves for new disclosure 'fresh from the Word.'"—Walter Brueggemann, *Introduction to the Old Testament*, 2nd ed. (Louisville, Ky.: Westminster John Knox Press, 2012), 10.

seeks to offer choices—a number of helpful suggestions for leading a successful Bible study using IBS.

How Should I Teach IBS?

1. Explore the Format

There is a wealth of information in IBS, perhaps more than you can use in one session. In this case, more is better. IBS has been designed to give you a well-stocked buffet of content and teachable insights. Pick and choose what suits your group's needs. Perhaps you will want to split units into two or more sessions, or combine units into a single session.

Perhaps you will decide to use only a portion of a unit and then move on to the next unit. *There is not a structured theme or teaching focus to each unit that must be followed for IBS to be used.* Rather, IBS offers the flexibility to adjust to whatever suits your context.

A recent survey of both professional and volunteer church educators revealed that their number-one concern was that Bible study materials be teacher-friendly.

> "The more we bring to the Bible, the more we get from the Bible." —William Barclay, *A Beginner's Guide to the New Testament* (Louisville, Ky.: Westminster John Knox Press, 1995), vii.

IBS is indeed teacher-friendly in two important ways. First, since IBS provides abundant content and a flexible design, teachers can shape the lessons creatively, responding to the needs of the group and employing a wide variety of teaching methods. Second, those who wish more specific suggestions for planning the sessions can find them at the Westminster John Knox Press Web site (**www.wjkbooks.com**). Here, you can access a study guide with teaching suggestions for each IBS unit as well as helpful quotations, selections from Bible dictionaries and encyclopedias, and other teaching helps.

IBS is not only teacher-friendly but also discussion-friendly. Given the opportunity, most adults and young people relish the chance to talk about the kind of issues raised in IBS. The secret, then, is to determine what works with your group, what will get them to talk. Several good methods for stimulating discussion are presented in this *Leader's Guide,* and once you learn your group, you can apply one of these methods and get the group discussing the Bible and its relevance in their lives.

The format of every IBS unit consists of several features:

a. Body of the Unit. This is the main content, consisting of interesting and informative commentary on the passage and scholarly insight into the biblical text and its significance for Christians today.

b. Sidebars. These are boxes that appear scattered throughout the body of the unit, with maps, photos, quotations, and intriguing ideas. Some sidebars can be identified quickly by a symbol, or icon, that helps the reader know what type of information can be found in that sidebar. There are icons for illustrations, key terms, pertinent quotes, and more.

c. Want to Know More? Each unit includes a "Want to Know More?" section that guides learners who wish to dig deeper and consult other resources. If your church library does not have the resources mentioned, you can look up the information in other standard Bible dictionaries, encyclopedias, and handbooks, or you can find much of this information at the Westminster John Knox Press Web site (see last page of this Guide).

d. Questions for Reflection. The unit ends with questions to help the learners think more deeply about the biblical passage and its pertinence for today. These questions are provided as examples only, and teachers are encouraged both to develop their own list of questions and to gather questions from the group. These discussion questions do not usually have specific "correct" answers. Again, the flexibility of IBS allows you to use these questions at the end of the group time, at the beginning, interspersed throughout, or not at all.

> "On the very first occasion when someone stood up in public to tell people about Jesus, he made it very clear: this message is for everyone. That message is as true today as it was then."—N. T. Wright, *Matthew for Everyone*, Part 2 (Louisville, Ky.: Westminster John Knox Press, 2004), ix.

2. Select a Teaching Method

Here are ten suggestions. The format of IBS allows you to choose what direction you will take as you plan to teach. Only you will know how your lesson should best be designed for your group. Some adult groups prefer the lecture method, while others prefer a high level of free-ranging discussion. Many youth groups like interaction, activity, the use of music, and the chance to talk about their own experiences and feelings. Here is a list of a few possible approaches. Let your own creativity add to the list!

a. Let's Talk about What We've Learned. In this approach, all group members are requested to read the scripture passage and the IBS unit before the group meets. Ask the group members to make notes about the main issues, concerns, and questions they see in the passage. When the group meets, these notes are collected, shared, and discussed. This method depends, of course, on the group's willingness to do some "homework."

b. What Do We Want and Need to Know? This approach begins by having the whole group read the scripture passage together. Then, drawing from your study of the IBS, you, as the teacher, write on a board or flip chart two lists:

(1) Things we should know to better understand this passage (content information related to the passage, for example, historical insights about political contexts, geographical landmarks, economic nuances, etc.), and

> "Although small groups can meet for many purposes and draw upon many different resources, the one resource which has shaped the life of the Church more than any other throughout its long history has been the Bible." —Roberta Hestenes, *Using the Bible in Groups* (Philadelphia: Westminster Press, 1983), 14.

(2) Four or five "important issues we should talk about regarding this passage" (with implications for today—how the issues in the biblical context continue into today, for example, issues of idolatry or fear).

Allow the group to add to either list, if they wish, and use the lists to lead into a time of learning, reflection, and discussion. This approach is suitable for those settings where there is little or no advanced preparation by the students.

c. Hunting and Gathering. Start the unit by having the group read the scripture passage together. Then divide the group into smaller clusters (perhaps having as few as one person), each with a different assignment. Some clusters can discuss one or more of the "Questions for Reflection." Others can look up key terms or people in a Bible dictionary or track down other biblical references found in the body of the unit. After the small clusters have had time to complete their tasks, gather the entire group again and lead them through the study material, allowing each cluster to contribute what it learned.

d. From Question Mark to Exclamation Point. This approach begins with contemporary questions and then moves to the biblical content as a response to those questions. One way to do this is for you to ask the group, at the beginning of the class, a rephrased version of one or more of the "Questions for Reflection" at the end of the study unit. For example, one of the questions at the end of the unit on Exodus 3:1–4:17 in the IBS *Exodus* volume reads,

> Moses raised four protests, or objections, to God's call. Contemporary people also raise objections to God's call. In what ways are these similar to Moses' protests? In what ways are they different?

This question assumes familiarity with the biblical passage about Moses, so the question would not work well before the group has explored the passage. However, try rephrasing this question as an opening exercise; for example:

Here is a thought experiment: Let's assume that God, who called people in the Bible to do daring and risky things, still calls people today to tasks of faith and courage. In the Bible, God called Moses from a burning bush and called Isaiah in a moment of ecstatic worship in the Temple. How do you think God's call is experienced by people today? Where do you see evidence of people saying "yes" to God's call? When people say "no" or raise an objection to God's call, what reasons do they give (to themselves, to God)?

Posing this or a similar question at the beginning will generate discussion and raise important issues, and then it can lead the group into an exploration of the biblical passage as a resource for thinking even more deeply about these questions.

e. Let's Go to the Library. From your church library, your pastor's library, or other sources, gather several good commentaries on the book of the Bible you are studying. Among the trustworthy commentaries are those in the Interpretation series (Westminster John Knox Press) and the Westminster Bible Companion series (Westminster John Knox Press). Divide your groups into smaller clusters and give one commentary to each cluster (one or more of the clusters can be given the IBS volume instead of a full-length commentary). Ask each cluster to read the biblical passage you are studying and then to read the section of the commentary that covers that passage (if your group is large, you may want to make photocopies of the commentary material with proper permission, of course). The task of each cluster is to name the two or three most important insights they discover about the biblical passage by reading and talking together about the commentary material. When you reassemble the larger group to share these insights, your group will gain not only a variety of insights about the passage but also a sense that differing views of the same text are par for the course in biblical interpretation.

f. Working Creatively Together. Begin with a creative group task, tied to the main thrust of the study. For example, if the study is on the Ten Commandments, a parable, or a psalm, have the group rewrite the Ten Commandments, the parable, or the psalm in contemporary language. If the passage is an epistle, have the group write a letter to their own congregation. Or if the study is a narrative, have the group role-play the characters in the story or write a page describing the story from the point of view of one of the characters. After completion of the task, read and discuss the biblical passage, asking for interpretations and applications from the group and tying in IBS material as it fits the flow of the discussion.

g. Singing Our Faith. Begin the session by singing (or reading) together a hymn that alludes to the biblical passage being studied (or to the theological themes in the passage). For example, if you are studying the unit from the IBS volume on Psalm 121, you can sing "I to the Hills Will Lift My Eyes," "Sing Praise to God, Who Reigns Above," or another hymn based on Psalm 121. Let the group reflect on the thoughts and feelings evoked by the hymn, then move to the biblical passage, allowing the biblical text and the IBS material to underscore, clarify, refine, and deepen the discussion stimulated by the hymn. If you are ambitious, you may ask the group to write a new hymn at the end of the study! (Many hymnals have indexes in the back or companion volumes that help the user match hymns to scripture passages or topics.)

h. Fill in the Blanks. In order to help the learners focus on the content of the biblical passage, at the beginning of the session ask each member of the group to read the biblical passage and fill out a brief questionnaire about the details of the passage (provide a copy for each learner or write the questions on the board). For example, if you are studying the unit in the IBS *Matthew* volume on Matthew 22:1–14, the questionnaire could include questions such as the following:

—In this story, Jesus compares the kingdom of heaven to what?
—List the various responses of those who were invited to the king's banquet but who did not come.
—When his invitation was rejected, how did the king feel? What did the king do?
—In the second part of the story, when the king saw a man at the banquet without a wedding garment, what did the king say? What did the man say? What did the king do?
—What is the saying found at the end of this story?

Gather the group's responses to the questions and perhaps encourage discussion. Then lead the group through the IBS material, helping the learners to understand the meanings of these details and the significance of the passage for today. Feeling creative? Instead of a fill-in-the-blanks questionnaire, create a crossword puzzle from names and words in the biblical passage.

i. Get the Picture. In this approach, stimulate group discussion by incorporating a painting, photograph, or other visual object into the lesson. You can begin by having the group examine and comment on this visual, or you can introduce the visual later in the lesson—it depends on the object used. If, for example, you are studying the unit Exodus 3:1–4:17 in the IBS *Exodus* volume, you may want to view Paul Koli's very colorful painting *The Burning Bush*. Two sources for this painting are *The Bible through Asian Eyes*, edited by Masao Takenaka and Ron O'Grady (National City, Calif.: Pace Publishing Co., 1991), and *Imaging the Word: An Arts and Lectionary Resource*, vol. 3, edited by Susan A. Blain (Cleveland: United Church Press, 1996).

j. Now Hear This. Especially if your class is large, you may want to use the lecture method. As the teacher, you prepare a presentation on the biblical passage, using as many resources as you have available plus your own experience, but following the content of the IBS unit as a guide. You can make the lecture even more lively by asking the learners at various points along the way to refer to the visuals and quotes found in the "sidebars." A place can be made for questions (like the ones at the end of the unit)—either at the close of the lecture or at strategic points along the way.

> "It is a mistake to look to the Bible to close a discussion; the Bible seeks to open one."—William Sloane Coffin, *Credo* (Louisville, Ky.: Westminster John Knox Press, 2004), 145.

3. Keep These Teaching Tips in Mind

There are no surefire guarantees for a teaching success. However, the following suggestions can increase the chances for a successful study:

a. Always Know Where the Group Is Headed. Take ample time beforehand to prepare the material. Know the main points of the study, and know the destination. Be flexible, and encourage discussion, but don't lose sight of where you are headed.

b. Ask Good Questions; Don't Be Afraid of Silence. Ideally, a discussion blossoms spontaneously from the reading of the scripture. But more often than not, a discussion must be drawn from the group members by a series of well-chosen questions. After asking each question, give the group members time to answer. Let them think, and don't be threatened by a season of silence. Don't feel that every question must have an answer and that as leader, you must supply every answer. Facilitate discussion by getting the group members to cooperate with each other. Sometimes the original question can be restated. Sometimes it is helpful to ask a follow-up question like "What makes this a hard question to answer?"

Ask questions that encourage explanatory answers. Try to avoid questions that can be answered simply "Yes" or "No." Rather than asking, "Do you think Moses was frightened by the burning bush?" ask, "What do you think Moses was feeling and experiencing as he stood before the burning bush?" If group members answer with just one word, ask a follow-up question like "Why do you think this is so?" Ask questions about their feelings and opinions, mixed within questions about facts or details. Repeat their responses or restate their response to reinforce their contributions to the group.

> "The whole purpose of the Bible, it seems to me, is to convince people to set the written word down in order to become living words in the world for God's sake. For me, this willing conversion of ink back to blood is the full substance of faith." —Barbara Brown Taylor, *Leaving Church: A Memoir of Faith* (New York: HarperOne, 2007), 107.

Most studies can generate discussion by asking open-ended questions. Depending on the group, several types of questions can work. Some groups will respond well to content questions that can be answered from reading the IBS comments or the biblical passage. Others will respond well to questions about feelings or thoughts. Still others will respond to questions that challenge them to new thoughts or that may not have exact answers. Be sensitive to the group's dynamic in choosing questions.

Some suggested questions are: What is the point of the passage? Who are the main characters? Where is the tension in the story? Why does it say (this) _____, and not (that) _____? What raises questions for you? What terms need defining? What are the new ideas? What doesn't make sense? What bothers or troubles you about this passage? What keeps you from living the truth of this passage?

c. Don't Settle for the Ordinary. There is nothing like a surprise. Think of special or unique ways to present the ideas of the study. Upset the applecart of the ordinary. Even though the passage may be familiar, look for ways to introduce suspense. Remember that a little mystery can capture the imagination. Change your routine.

Along with the element of surprise, humor can open up a discussion. Don't be afraid to laugh. A well-chosen joke or cartoon may present the central theme in a way that a lecture would have stymied.

Sometimes a passage is too familiar. No one speaks up because everyone feels that all that could be said has been said. Choose an unfamiliar translation from which to read, or if the passage is from a Gospel, compare the story across two or more Gospels and note differences. It is amazing what insights can be drawn from seeing something strange in what was thought to be familiar.

d. Feel Free to Supplement the IBS Resources with Other Material. Consult other commentaries or resources. Tie in current events with the lesson. Scour newspapers or magazines for stories that touch on the issues of the study. Sometimes the lyrics of a song, or a section of prose from a well-written novel, will be just the right seasoning for the study. The Thoughtful Christian (www .TheThoughtfulChristian.com) has a multitude of Bible study and teaching material available.

e. And Don't Forget to Check the Web. You can download a free study guide from our Web site (**www.wjkbooks.com**). Each study guide includes several possibilities for applying the teaching methods suggested above for individual IBS units.

f. Stay Close to the Biblical Text. Don't forget that the goal is to learn the Bible. Return to the text again and again. Avoid making the mistake of reading the passage only at the beginning of the study, and then wandering away to comments on top of comments from that point on. Trust in the power

> "The Bible is literature, but it is much more than literature. It is the holy book of Jews and Christians, who find there a manifestation of God's presence." —Kathleen Norris, *The Psalms* (New York: Riverhead Books, 1997), xxii.

and presence of the Holy Spirit to use the truths of the passage to work within the lives of the study participants.

What If I Am Using IBS in Personal Bible Study?

If you are using IBS in your personal Bible study, you can experiment and explore a variety of ways. You may choose to read straight through the study without giving any attention to the sidebars or other features. Or you may find yourself interested in a question or unfamiliar with a key term, and you can allow the sidebars "Want to Know More?" and "Questions for Reflection" to lead you into deeper learning on these issues. Perhaps you will want to have a few commentaries or a Bible dictionary available to pursue what interests you. As was suggested in one of the teaching methods above, you may want to begin with the questions at the end, and then read the Bible passage followed by the IBS material. Trust the IBS resources to provide good and helpful information, and then follow your interests!

Want to Know More?

Studies at The Thoughtful Christian

These studies, which are available at www.TheThoughtfulChristian.com, will help with questions about Bible study, Bible basics, and the development of the Bible:

- "Bible 101," by John A. Cairns
- "Biblical Interpretation 101," by W. Eugene March
- "How to Study a Bible Passage," by Donald L. Griggs
- "The Importance of Context" and "Tools for Bible Study," by Gary W. Light
- "Types of Literature in the Bible" and "When and Why the Bible Was Written," by Emily Cheney
- "Which Bible Should I Buy?" by Steven M. Sheeley

Other Helpful Resources

- *The Bible from Scratch: The Old Testament for Beginners*, by Donald L. Griggs (Louisville, Ky.: Westminster John Knox Press, 2002) and *The Bible from Scratch: The New Testament for Beginners*, by Donald L. Griggs (Louisville, Ky.: Westminster John Knox Press, 2003)
- *How the Bible Came to Be*, by John Barton (Louisville, Ky.: Westminster John Knox Press, 1997)
- *Using the Bible in Groups*, by Roberta Hestenes (Louisville, Ky.: Westminster John Knox Press, 1983)

To download a free IBS study guide,

visit our Web site at

www.wjkbooks.com

CPSIA information can be obtained
at www.ICGtesting.com
Printed in the USA
LVHW041105090223
739072LV00021B/436